Praise for Mike Foster by top level executives . . .

"Wow! You are like the Tiger Woods of IT Best Practices!"

– Tom, CFO, Cincinnati, OH

"I think it is a testament to Mike that my IT people want him back for another review! They want to show him what they've accomplished and find out new best practices in IT."

*– Bill Litjen, President, GS Levine
Insurance Services, San Diego, CA*

"Mike always took the time to explain (in non-technical terms) what we needed to improve and why we needed to change things. This helped define our challenges and fine tune our solutions—with incredible results."

– Donna, P.M. and Manager of IT, Bridgewater, NJ

"What really impressed me was your professionalism. Your advice and suggestions were to-the point and they helped us get on the right track. Everything you offered us exceeded my expectations."

– Tony, CFO, Truckee, CA

"Wow! I was amazed by the amount of custom information included in the program. Its timing was perfect, and Mike's knowledge was excellent. I definitely increased my understanding of the Internet and the growing number of security issues IT must continue to tackle."

– Jim, CEO, Appleton, WI

"Mike does a terrific job of walking the balance between business and IT issues. I plan to implement several of the suggestions he offered, and I now understand the urgency in having an IT audit."

– Larry, CIO, Lenexa, KS

"Not only are you well informed, but you are able to communicate your information on multiple levels at the same time—to IT professionals and to the CEOs."

– Ed, Information Systems Manager, Buffalo, NY

"I was amazed not only by the depth of your program, but also by the fact you kept everyone involved in the subject. I appreciated your pitch to the CEOs, many of whom are not informed enough to understand or fight for IT security."

– Debbie, CIO, Palm Beach, FL

THE
SECURE
CEO

How To Protect Your Computer Systems, Your Company, and Your Job

"Plain English Information Every CEO & Key Executive Needs to Know about Network Security and IT Best Practices to Stop Hackers and Slackers."

Mike Foster

For additional copies contact:
The Foster Institute
PO Box 610146
Dallas, TX 75261-0146 USA
Phone: 800-657-7107 or 214-269-1204
www.FosterInstitute.com

Published by:
Prime Concepts Group Publishing
1807 S. Eisenhower St.
Wichita, KS 67209-2810 USA

Publisher's Cataloging-in-Publication

Foster, Mike, 1965-
    The secure CEO : how to protect your computer
systems, your company, and your job / Mike Foster.
    p. cm.
    "Plain English information every CEO & key executive
needs to know about network security and IT best
practices to stop hackers and slackers."
    LCCN 2007938848
    ISBN-13: 978-0-9715578-0-2
    ISBN-10: 0-9715578-0-2

    1. Business enterprises--Computer networks--
Management. 2. Information technology--Management.
3. Information technology--Security measures.   I. Title.

HD30.37.F67 2007   658'.05
                          QBI07-600284

Contents

Acknowledgements

Primarily, thank you to my loving and understanding wife. She knows how busy I am, and supports me in my mission, every day, to make the world a more secure and more productive place through helping organizations with their IT practices.

I wish to thank the many mentors who have helped me learn the information that is contained within. Some of you I communicate with daily, some of you we haven't talked in years, and I've never met some of you (authors of great books, and even people who died centuries ago who's wisdom lives on in books).

Thank you also to the many many clients who's executives and IT professionals alike have taken the time to explain "your exact situation," how you are dealing with it this far, what has worked, what hasn't worked, and for being open to trying the recommendations you receive from the consulting.

Thank you too those of you that have referred me to your friends and associates.

And, finally, thank you—the reader—who will absorb this information and use it to both secure your information and also get the most out of your IT investments.

– Mike Foster

Introduction

Ask any executive and they'll tell you that using technology to increase profits and productivity is very important these days. And even though technology is supposed to save us a lot of time, the reality is that the majority of business people feel that technology also brings burdens into their lives.

When I speak to audiences about technology, I just mention the word "e-mail" and a lot of people wince and groan. So I know that technology isn't always a fun topic. One of my audience members summed it up perfectly one time when he said, "You know what, Mike? Technology is amazing. It lets me solve all kinds of problems I've never even had before."

And yes, that's how we feel a lot of the time. That's why my goal of this book is to help you understand technology a little better so you can use it for the benefit it was meant to give you.

The good news is that you don't have to be an "IT geek" to understand technology. Anyone, yes *anyone*, can become more aware of IT issues.

When I go into companies, especially small ones with 700 or fewer computers, I see some common IT problems. One company that comes to mind is a wonderful firm in the Midwest. They started out small and over time grew quite substantially. When I met with them and looked over their IT department, they were in the midst of their growth spurt. They claimed to "hate computers," and it showed. I looked at the network, and sure enough, it reminded me of how teenagers would set up a network in their garage. In the back of my mind I thought, "No wonder this network isn't working for them."

So I pulled the IT person aside and asked him, "By the way, where did you get your IT training? Who taught you this stuff?"

He looked at me with a puzzled look and said, "No one. I went to college and studied music. I'm a concert pianist."

I then asked him how he got into IT, and he said, "I started out when the company was really small. We got our first computer, and I was the only one here who even knew how to use the mouse. So the owner said that I was now in charge of IT. I've been here ever since." (I hear similar statements a lot.)

He had managed to study and learn along the way, but the biggest problem was that he was lacking some important information. Additionally, along the way, some less-than-adequate IT consultants he hired had fed him erroneous information. Fortunately, I was able to mentor him and coach him, and he learned a lot of important things about changing the network around. The information I gave him would have been simple to people who've had extensive formal IT training, but to him, it was all new information. As such, their network got a lot better.

The point of this story is that even if someone started out in the mail room, if he or she now has to interact with technology in any way, offer that person some training. Let your people get certified in something you use. For most companies, having people certified as a Microsoft Certified Systems Engineer is a good start, as I would think that you have at least one Microsoft Windows server in your organization.

As an executive, you are already aware that technology is nice; however, creativity and relationships are what got you where you are today. And those are the two things that will keep you successful in the future. Realize that technology is a powerful tool to help with those things.

That's why the information in this book will not only teach you lots about what you need to know to keep your company safe from IT breaches, but it will also help you better relate to your IT professionals so you can work together as a team to keep the company moving forward.

My goal with this book is to give you a lot of tools and strategies you can start using right now. Throughout this book I'm going to give you web sites to go to and products to investigate. I do my best to keep this information updated, but sometimes things in business change quickly. So if a certain product or web site is no longer available, be sure to contact me for updates.

At the end of each chapter you'll see Action Items. These are specific things for you to do to help you implement the information in the chapter. We all know that information is useless if you don't implement it, and I created these Action Items to give you a head start on your IT security issues.

I also recommend that you put a timeline to your IT objectives. Too many times we put important things on the "back burner" so we can put out fires. But putting out fires is an inefficient use of anyone's time. You're better off putting the practices in place that will keep the fires from starting in the first place.

Realize that I am very much an "IT professional," but I have also functioned in executive roles. Today, I enjoy being able to give executives a window into the "IT professional's world" and visa-versa. The world of IT isn't just about pocket protectors and glasses with tape in the middle, although sometimes that is part of it.

When I visit with IT professionals, I talk about having them seem like they are the Maytag Man in those old TV commercials, meaning that as far as IT goes, it would be wonderful if they could just be sitting there with nothing to do because the network is taking care of itself. Of course, we all realize that will never happen. Technology is forever changing, and IT professionals need to be learning, researching, and making decisions about what the next strategic step is for the company.

The problem is that far too many IT professionals are just running around putting out fires most of their days, and the learning, researching, and strategizing rarely get done. This busy-ness may feel comfortable to an IT professional, and allow him or her to feel some "fulfillment" at the end of the day. It may even impress the boss to see the IT professionals "getting so much done." The reality is, they (the IT professionals) are stealing from themselves and the company.

A lot of IT professionals are real good at showing people how a computer can make their job easier. But sometimes we IT professionals forget to go to the mirror, look at ourselves, and say, "Hey, here's what you could do Mr. or Ms. IT professional (meaning yourself) to make the job easier."

The goal of this book is to get your computers to the point where they take care of themselves. Now, your IT professional is never going to look like the Maytag repairman. However, he or she will be able to be proactive and do things that help your network, streamline it, and make it better. This then enables your IT staff to flourish and protect your company instead of running around and putting out fires. But to get to that point, you need some sort of central management tool, which we'll discuss at various points throughout this book.

The bottom line is that the more you, the executive, know about technology and IT issues, and the more training and support you give your IT team, the better your company will be. You certainly want a better and more secure company, don't you? Well then, keep reading…we have a lot of ground to cover.

CHAPTER 1

How Secure Are You?

Most CEOs are certainly interested in their company's security. That's why they install security systems in their office, keep valuable documents in a fireproof safe or at a secure offsite location, and do thorough background checks on all new hires. But what about IT security? What about all that proprietary and confidential data stored on the company's computers? How safe is that? For most CEOs, the answer is "not very."

Why is IT security so important these days? Consider this: Recently, the University of Southern California had a problem where 270,000 records were lost. Then, in December 2006, UCLA announced that they lost 800,000 records. (Yes, for all you UCLA fans, UCLA beat USC again.) All joking aside, the records that were lost contained not just students' names, but also their social security numbers.

In another example, a major credit card processing company had a security breach that exposed 40 million credit card numbers to hackers. 40 million! Chances are high that one of your credit card numbers was among the lot.

So what's the big deal with these kinds of security breaches? Identity theft. (We'll talk more about identity theft later.

For now just realize that having your identity stolen is no laughing matter.)

From a business perspective, imagine what it would be like for the University of Southern California and UCLA to have to notify everyone about the security breach. Imagine having to be one of the call center reps at the credit card processing company after the notification of the security breach went out to customers. That would not be a fun task for any company.

Now, think about your own company for a moment. How would it be if you had to notify your customers, your employees, and maybe even your vendors that you had a security breach? Most CEOs cringe at the idea.

To complicate matters, some companies use outside services to help them keep up with day-to-day functions, such as accounting or payroll. If that outside service provider has a security breach and they notify you of the problem, then it's your responsibility to notify your customers, employees, and vendors that their information may have been compromised. And even though it wasn't your company that had the breach, but rather a company you relied on for a particular service, who do you think your customers, employees, and/ or vendors will be upset with? That's right...you. People tend to "shoot the messenger."

That's why you need to make sure that whoever is processing any of your data has ample IT security measures in place.

Realize that depending on your unique combination of federal, state, and local laws, you may be mandated to report any kind of IT security breaches to the people involved. Additionally, you may be subject to some form of liability, such as needing to provide credit protection services and/or needing to pay for damages if someone does suffer any problems from the security breach.

It's no wonder then that some companies purposely choose not to report security breaches. Those who have gone this route say they do so hoping that no one finds out, because the negative publicity would kill their company. Others have even revealed that their legal advisors told them to withhold the information, again stating that if they announced it like they should, it would devastate their business and force them to close. It's interesting that a legal advisor would actually advise someone to break the law, but that is what happens sometimes.

Going back to our credit card processing company and university examples, do you suppose that the heads of these organizations thought their information was secure? Of course they did. I highly doubt any business leader would knowingly allow a security breach to happen. Yet, thinking you're secure is not the same as actually being secure. This book will help you bridge the gap.

I'd hate for your company to end up like the credit card processing company example. After they notified their customers of the breach, they lost every single one of their clients—not one stayed with them. Few companies can survive such a setback.

Furthermore, larger companies can rebound better and quicker from major setbacks, such as a data breech. Smaller companies, however, have a much more difficult time rebounding because they often lack the resources required to see them through the troubled times.

To get started on the road to better security, ask yourself the following questions:

1. When was the last time you audited your security?

2. When was the last time you talked with your IT support people, in-house or outsourced, about your IT security exposure?

3. Does your organization have a strong password policy, or is the culture so relaxed that more than one person might know a specific password to a user's account?

4. If you carry a laptop with you, how secure are you when you connect at the hotels and airports during your travels?

5. How big a deal would it be if hackers managed to shut down your network for three days? For a week? For even longer?

6. Do you have any company secrets, such as your formula for doing business and/or pricing information, that you want to protect?

7. Have you or has anyone you know ever been affected by a data security breach of some kind?

Finally, and this is a big one, are your computers "earning their keep"?

By that I mean, are they adequate for today's needs. One way to have computers earn their keep is to have them increase productivity. These days, one of the best ways to increase the speed of a computer is to add chip memory, commonly referred to as RAM. Too many companies have older computers that are running slowly. When you add the security tools mentioned in this book, the computers may run even slower unless you provide them with enough memory. As your IT professional will tell you, these days 512 Meg is a bare minimum and 1 Gig of RAM is a much better amount of RAM for existing PCs. It is a good idea to order 2 Gigs of RAM with new machines. Those are fairly standard RAM sizes as of the printing of this book and will work well for the majority of companies.

Be honest with your answers. The more honest you are with yourself and your company's state of security, the better protected you can be in the future.

Action Item: Read on, and start tightening up your security today!

CHAPTER 2

How Your IT Department Affects Security

B y now you may be thinking, "Hey…that could never happen at my company. I have an IT guy (or gal) on staff who keeps up with all that stuff." And if you do have a dedicated person or even team of experienced IT staff, then that's wonderful. But let me explain what often happens in companies . . .

Many CEOs and even many IT professionals believe that security is part of IT's job. And that makes complete sense. But here's what can happen. If you go to your IT professional and ask him "Are we secure?" he isn't going to hear exactly what you asked. If he believes that security is part of his job, he will filter what he hears. What he actually hears you ask is, "Are you doing your job?"

Realize that almost everyone has filters on their hearing. I have filters on my hearing. My wife points it out to me all the time.

So going back to our IT guy, if he hears the question "Are you doing your job?" how do you think he's going to respond? Chances are he's going to say, "You bet." You, the CEO, then walk off, thinking you're secure, until some kind of breach happens in your company.

Many CEOs have no idea how insecure their company's data actually is. I see it over and over every day with the companies I help. So what I want to give you in this book are specific questions you can ask your IT professionals. Rather than ask your IT professionals "Do we handle X?" I want you to phrase your questions as "How do we handle X?" There's a big difference between the two phrases, and you'll get much better answers using the latter approach.

Additionally, by using proper phrasing for your questions, your IT professional is going to be thrilled. He or she is going to be very excited that you understand IT's plight. Your questions will make it apparent that you don't always expect to see your IT professional working on someone's computer or printer, and that sometimes they have to do "behind the scenes" work that isn't glamorous.

This is important, because unfortunately, in a lot of organizations when you ask your IT professional "Are we secure?" and he or she answers "You bet," the IT professional walks away and thinks to him or herself, "Oh, no, I just told my boss that we're secure. I'd better go fix the firewall. There's been a problem in the firewall, a known vulnerability in the firmware that's been there for six months. I need to fix it today."

So the IT professional heads back to the server room to fix the firewall. But on the way, Mary Lou, one of the administrative assistants, grabs the IT professional and says,

"My printer isn't working. Can you fix it?" Now the IT professional has to make a decision. Does he fix Mary Lou's printer, or does he fix the firewall that's going to affect the whole company?

Keep in mind this is the little printer that came for free when the company bought Mary Lou's desktop. The IT professional set it up on Mary Lou's desk, and Mary Lou just loves it. And the last time that free little printer broke (which was only a few days ago), the IT professional suggested that maybe Mary Lou get out of her chair, walk down the hall, and get her printouts from the network printer. When word spread that the IT professional said that, he got chastised, because after all, IT is supposed to fix "stuff."

So what do you think this IT professional does? Does he fix Mary Lou's printer (something everyone will see him working on), or does he fix the firewall (something nobody has a clue that it's even having a problem)?

Of course he's going to fix Mary Lou's printer. Not only that, but if this IT professional has a high need for approval, which many people do, which scenario is going to give him more gratification? If he fixes Mary Lou's printer, she'll get excited and say, "Thank you, thank you...you're my hero." If he fixes the firewall, no one will say anything. There's no pat on the back and no thank you's.

So Mary Lou's printer is going to get fixed. (By the way, the best thing you can do with those free printers that come with the workstation is to send them home with your employee. And tell them, "I don't want to ever see this printer again." Let them buy the supplies and deal with all the problems. Keep everyone on your network printers. Your IT professionals will thank you.)

So even though the IT professional knows the network needs to be secure, he chooses to fix the printer and vows to fix the firewall first thing tomorrow morning. As he drives home he thinks about how he's going to fix it. During his drive into work the next morning, he thinks, "I'm going to get the download, back up the router, and apply the patch. Then I'm going to test it. If everything's fine, we're good to go. It's only going to take me about ten or 15 minutes to do this. I'm going to do it first thing."

The IT professional walks into the office and heads back to the server room. But on the way, someone else grabs him and says, "One of the executives has lost the solitaire icon on his laptop. He's getting ready to leave for a business trip and says he'll go insane on the airplane without solitaire. Can you fix it before he leaves?"

So what do you think the IT professional is going to work on now? The lost solitaire icon for the executive, or the firewall? I guarantee the solitaire icon will win.

So the IT professional helps the executive and fixes the solitaire icon, all the while vowing to fix the firewall first thing tomorrow morning before everyone logs on. But what happens tomorrow? Another printer is down, or another icon is lost, or another mouse is broken…the list goes on.

If you suspect this may be happening in your company, rest assured you can break the cycle. One simple way is to give your IT professionals an hour a day to spend doing nothing but security stuff. Tell them that you want to be kept up to date on what they're doing security-wise, too. Why? Because not only will you be informed (which you should be), but your IT professionals will know that you're interested in what they're doing and that you appreciate their efforts. And that's the first step to better IT security.

Action Item: Give your IT staff the time they need to tend to the non-visible tasks that are essential for your company's security.

CHAPTER 3

The Cost of Security Breaches

When it comes to IT security, CEOs often tell me, "But, Mike, it doesn't matter. If someone really wants to get in and hack our system, they will." So these CEOs remain unprotected. Then, when something does happen, they wonder, "Why didn't somebody tell me this could happen? Now I'm losing my business." What a mess.

Exactly how costly could a security breach be to a company? I have a client on the East Coast that lost a third of a million dollars due to a security breach. And the interesting thing is that I met them a year and a half prior. At that time, they scheduled a security review for me to come in and look at their system. Then they would call me every few months and say, "We need to push it out. We're too busy. We need to push it out." Then one day I got the call where they said, "You have to get here as soon as you possibly can."

Fortunately, I had an appointment I could cancel on one of the days and I flew to their location. The entire flight I kept thinking, "If only they had had the review we could have prevented all this." But by the time I arrived it was too late. The damage had already been done. As it turned out, a hacker from China invaded their system and destroyed all their files.

When I tell this story, people wonder how the company could lose so much money just from destroyed files. They mistakenly believe that companies only lose money when their bank accounts get hacked into and drained. But because this company lost all their data, they were shut down for an entire week (and still paying employees' salaries). Additionally, they had to bring in an army of IT professionals to rebuild their system. Add to that the cost of all the lost sales (and the customers who decided not to do business with them anymore as a result), and you have a loss of a third of a million dollars.

But that's only the loss they've calculated. In reality, they also have costs that occur "after the fact." That is, their business stopped for a week and now they have to get it going again. So they have to do more marketing to regain customer confidence. They have to catch up on any work that's behind that they didn't finish prior to the security breach. They have to do the new work that's coming in. They have to field customer calls (some very angry customer calls). As you can see, this really snowballs. So if they really put their pen to it, they'd find out this security breach was more expensive than they had realized.

That's why you need to take time to analyze how much it would cost you if you were down for a certain amount of time. If your company can survive being down a week, then it's not as crucial to have standby servers. But if your company is in the situation where you'd be devastated not having email for an hour, then you do need to have standby servers, probably collocated, online, running all the time servers. The point is that you have to figure out what your exposure is, and then protect yourself accordingly. Don't overprotect, but don't under protect either.

The FBI knows that the cost of security breaches is a big deal. In 2006, the FBI partnered with 313 companies who agreed to be in a study about IT security. The companies came from various sectors, such as medical, education, transportation, manufacturing, and many more. Combined, these companies lost over $52 million due to various types of security breaches, including viruses, theft of proprietary information, network abuse, data sabotage, and much more. If you do the math, that's $167,000 plus per company, which is an expensive loss.

You certainly don't want to be part of that loss. The FBI asked these 313 companies why they believe more companies don't report their security losses. Well, 48 percent of the companies in the study said that negative publicity would hurt their stock or image. Another 36 percent said their competitors could use the information to their advantage. I'm sure you could think of many more reasons.

So the costs of IT security breaches are real and devastating to many companies. But realize that there's power in knowledge. That's why you need to know what your potential losses are. Only then can you take the proper steps to protect your company.

To that end, I recommend that every company create a Security Incident Management Plan. In this plan you will write exactly how you will:

- Identify security incidents
- Contact law enforcement if appropriate
- Notify anyone whose personal information may have been exposed
- Protect and gather appropriate evidence
- Clean up the problems
- Put appropriate monitoring in place
- Identify lessons learned to better protect the system

Find out more information at www.csrc.nist.gov/publications/nistpubs/800-61/sp800-61.pdf.

Action Item: Make a commitment to yourself to take the topic of IT security very seriously now and in the future.

CHAPTER 4

The Great Disconnect

Now that you know an overview of the problem and how it can harm your company, it's time to take the steps that can keep your company safe. One of the most important steps you can take is to learn how to communicate with your IT team.

Realize that of all the professional relationships that can make or break your business, your relationship with your IT support staff is one of the most critical. In fact, it's just as critical as is your relationship with your CPA, your banker, and even your attorney. When your IT staff feels supported and acknowledged, and when they're armed with the proper technology, they can single-handedly keep your company from losing data, losing work time, and losing customer confidence. Your IT staff can prevent you from being like my client on the East coast discussed in the previous chapter— the one who lost a third of a million dollars due to an IT security breach.

Many CEOs believe their IT staff is intimidated by them. In reality, it's simply that the IT professionals don't know how to sell an executive on what needs to get done. Think of the typical IT professional as the antithesis of your star salesperson. Your star salesperson knows the art of persuasion.

He or she knows how to make something important and meaningful to the listener.

Conversely, your typical IT professional can't always put into words why the new technology the company needs is important, even though it is *very* important. Rather than focus on the bottom line benefit the new technology will give the company, the IT professional drones on and on about all the cool features of the new technology. And what do you do as the CEO? Most likely, your eyes glaze over and your mind drifts to some other topic. Before long you're staring at your IT professional and you see his or her mouth moving, but you're not hearing a word.

While your IT professional is saying things like, "This tool will log people on the Internet," "This device will automatically back up our server," and "This gadget will encrypt our data," all you're thinking is, "Is this thing going to stop people from wasting time on the Internet?" "Will the tool protect us against sexual harassment lawsuits?" "Can this new technology help us outsmart our competition?" In other words, you don't care what it does day-to-day; you simply want to know what it will help you achieve long-term, preferably in terms of dollars and cents or productivity metrics.

So what's a CEO to do? Here are some suggestions to help you develop the relationship with your IT team and get them on the same page as you.

- The first and most obvious suggestion is to send your IT professionals to some communication training. I do a three-hour presentation about what the IT professionals wish the executives knew, and what the executives wish the IT professionals knew. It's a real eye-opener for both IT professionals and the executives they work with. You can get more information about it at www.fosterinstitute.com. There is also an expanded workshop for IT professionals that shows them project management skills as well as many other skills at www.supertechevent.com.

- Second, when you're talking with your IT professional and she drones on about the features of a new item, ask her point blank, "What is the ultimate benefit of this technology for the company?" Get your IT professionals in the habit of thinking in this manner.

- Send your IT professionals to project management training of some kind. Often IT professionals have to manage multiple projects that are behind schedule and over budget, yet few have formal project management training.

- Provide your IT professionals with some authority, but not too much. If the IT professional needs to tell someone, "I will fix your printer in a little while because the network server is about to crash," then the IT professional needs the authority to make that decision without being reprimanded later.

- Hold the IT professionals responsible for their actions and provide measurements to them so that they can see how effective they are at their jobs. Some companies choose to measure down-time, help desk requests, or other values that are easy to track.

- When you hire your next IT professional, seriously consider the person's people skills as well as technical aptitude. If the person's technical skills are lacking, but she has aptitude to learn more, you can send her to training for technical skills. But if her people skills are lacking, she won't change until she reaches a hurt level in her life that is so bad that she decides to change herself.

- Understand that many IT professionals have a personality of wanting to work with "things" rather than "people." That may or may not fit the culture of your company and the job position they are filling. Just don't try to force a round pin into a square hole.

- If you find that your staff reports that the IT professional is abrasive, and you want to stretch the IT professional into new areas of growth, try asking him how he "feels" about some specific issue you know is going on in your company. With some IT professionals, you may see a blank glazed over look. "Feel? What's that?" they may think. If and when your IT professional discovers his own feelings, the next step is to ask him, "How do you suppose Suzie might feel when you tell her ____?" Frankly, this task of helping recover an abrasive IT professional is generally not worth the effort, but if you have some kind of co-dependent rescuer fantasy you want to act upon, be my guest. Somebody needs to help these lost people identify their plight. I've had IT professionals look me in the eye and say, "This boss is as bad as all the other five bosses I've had over the past two years." They don't "get it" that they, the IT professionals, are the common denominator in those multiple lost jobs. If the IT professional resorts to making threats and ultimatums, show him the door. You cannot afford to have someone who "holds the keys to your company" the way an IT professional does making threats.

- When you want to show appreciation to an IT professional, be sure to find out what she really likes. It may be that having a second monitor on her desk would mean more than a $1,000 bonus. Or maybe she wants to upgrade her computer twice a year. The key is to ask and find out.

- Tell your IT staff not to try to impress you with big words and acronyms. Explain that patient explanations that focus on the bottom line result is what will impress you.

- Some IT professionals suffer since they are forced to wear so many hats. To perform good IT work, IT professionals need uninterrupted periods during the day to focus. Having three hours a day of uninterrupted time, even if split into three one hour periods, would seem like nirvana to some IT professionals.

Remember, as the CEO, it's your job to initiate open dialogue with everyone on your team, including your IT team. If you don't, you'll end up in a situation where your IT professionals will believe they can't come to you with issues that affect the company. They'll think, "I can't bring this up to the CEO. Sure, we need to fix the anti-virus problem, but he's not going to approve the $19 per machine cost to upgrade." Then you'll never know where your company's weaknesses are until it's too late.

Author and business leader Jack Welch brings up an interesting point. He talks about a "twisted chain of command." As he explains, "Far too often, crucial departments like IT and HR report to finance instead of the CEO." He gives an example of a company where an employee reveals, "I work for a company where the information technology department reports to the head of finance. He [the head of finance] never has time to evaluate IT projects, so IT gets attention only when there's a burning issue."

I've seen this same issue happen time and time again.

One that comes to mind immediately is a company on the West Coast that's now out of business. Their IT professional was going to Controller every month and explaining, "Our backup is not working. We have no backup. Do you understand that we have no backup? We need this $1,600 part to fix our backup." This particular Controller knew a little bit about technology. Now we've all learned that a little bit of knowledge can be dangerous. So the Controller replied, "I know we have a RAID array. That's enough for us right now. We won't approve the cost for the part." (A RAID array means you have an extra drive in your server, so that if one drive fails, the data is, usually, still available.) To that the IT guy kept saying, "No, a RAID array is not enough for us right now." And the Controller kept replying, "Yes it is. Now go away." Eventually the IT professional gave up.

Well, as you may have already suspected, they lost not one, but two drives one day, and the RAID array failed. As a result, the company went under. That was the only time I remember actually crying at a job site. I walked in and saw all those architects and their long faces. I started thinking about their families who were losing one of, if not the only, major income provider for the family. It was a very sad time, especially for something so ridiculous and that a $1,600 part would have fixed.

That's why you need to make sure you have a good dialogue with your IT professionals. And if your IT department does have to report to finance for some reason, make sure that finance does not ignore them. Arm finance with the same communication tools you give your IT professionals. Get the relationship between the two departments established. Make sure everyone is listening to each other so you can avoid potential disaster.

Action Item: If your IT professional is willing, send him or her to school to learn more about keeping your network secure. Companies learned a long time ago how important it is to educate their teams. IT is becoming so complicated that it is more like the medical field. Nobody would expect an eye surgeon to be an expert cardiologist as well. Allow your IT professional to outsource when necessary.

CHAPTER 5

Outsourcing Your IT

M any companies outsource their IT needs. That is, they don't have any internal IT staff and bring in outsiders to handle that aspect of their company.

Depending on your company and its size, outsourcing your IT may be a good decision. If you happen to be one of the many companies that outsources IT, I have a special assignment for you. Call your IT service provider and say, "I know we call you to come in and fix whatever's broken, but we'd like you to come in for a little extra time and see what else might need to be fixed that we haven't ever called you about."

Why do this? Because one of the problems with outsourcing your IT needs is that the IT professional comes in and just fixes what you called them for, and then they leave. This is actually in the IT provider's best interests, because it guarantees they'll have a steady amount of work from you.

However, you're better off having them come in, tighten up all the hatches, and get things running right.

Recently I was at a company in a southern state. This company outsources 100 percent of their IT needs to a local firm. They have 30 machines and pay approximately, $200,000 a year to the IT firm. That's a lot of money for 30 machines.

Even though this company outsources their IT, they have an IT professional there on site at least four days a week, and more often five. As I watched this IT professional work, I saw that all he was doing was running around and putting out fires. So I sat down and had a security review with the person. We looked at the systems and everything else.

During the first part of the review, where I sit with the IT professional and we have a tabletop discussion, he gave me lip service, saying, "Oh, yeah, we do that."

But when we went out into the business and started looking at the servers and the workstations, I quickly learned that everything he told me during the tabletop meeting was a bunch of nonsense. Some of it he knew was nonsense, and he was hoping I wouldn't notice. But for much of it, he truly wasn't aware of some of the problems we found.

For example, the computer the HR Director used had six spyware Trojans on it, numerous viruses, and it hadn't been updated with something called Microsoft Update since it was installed two years ago. Of all the computers to have vulnerable to hackers, HR's computer would give unscrupulous people lots of data to work with.

Later, I met with the CEO of the company and asked him, "Do you trust your IT service provider?"

He replied, "No, not really."

I said, "Well, the guy here today is very competent. Why don't you let him go ahead and put the needed patches and tools on your computers?" And I gave him a very detailed list of about 27 pages explaining what needed to be done. I also explained that once he got all these fixes in place, he would no longer need the IT provider there as often and would save well over half to three-quarters of the money he had been spending on IT needs.

That got his attention.

So by all means outsource your IT if you need to; just make sure you allow the IT professionals to do their job and keep your computers safe and clean.

Action Item: If you haven't had a vendor-neutral third party evaluate your IT systems recently, do so now. Yearly is a good frequency for this kind of evaluation.

CHAPTER 6

Pros and Cons of Outsourced IT

I know this chapter is titled "Pros and Cons," but rather than end the chapter on the downside of things, I'd like to do the pros last so I can leave you with positive images of outsourced IT. Again, outsourcing your IT needs is a great option for many companies. I created and operated a company that was "outsourced IT" for many organizations for more than ten years. The key is to beware of the company you're working with. Check them out and make sure it's a company you feel confident being supported by.

So first the cons.

When it comes to cons, I always remember the company in Florida that I helped, where the CEO actually spent about half an hour telling me how I wasn't going to find anything there during the security review, but he just wanted to be extra sure. After I finished meeting with him, I went out into his office and looked at his network. I like to do a head to toe examination, which I learned earlier in my life as a paramedic. So I started the Internet working, and then I checked the router. Everything looked updated.

Then I looked at the back of the firewall appliance and I saw that there was only one cord plugged in. Guess which cord? If you guessed the power cord, you're right. I traced the Ethernet cable and found that their router went straight into their corporate switch, meaning they had the tools to protect themselves, but the tools weren't hooked up and his company was vulnerable.

Now this is a company that makes a product that is not only patented, but it's also the only one of its kind on the market. The CEO told me stories about people standing in the parking lot with cameras taking pictures of everybody going in and out of his office, hoping that they can find somebody with an open blueprint or some other information that would reveal how their product is made. So this is a company that needs to be secure.

When I showed the CEO what I found, he turned beet-red. I then asked the CFO, who is the go-to person in the office for IT matters, "Did you know about this?" She replied, "Oh, yeah. Whenever that thing's hooked up, we can't send or receive e-mail, so our outsource people said we should just unhook it, and we did."

I explained that their outsource IT professionals did not give them good advice. All they needed to do was open up the ports so e-mail could come through. I then said, "Well, were they going to come back and help you fix this?" She said they were. So I continued, "Well, tell me this was yesterday when they unhooked it, and that they'll be back later today to hook it back up."

"Oh, no," she said, "It's been about six months."

Yikes! But this is the kind of atrocities I see. At that same company I found out that their domain administrator password was the one-word name of their company. So in other words, if the company was named Tekco, their password to get into their domain as the administrator who has access to everything was also Tekco. Talk about a hacker attack just waiting to happen.

As it turns out, this particular outsource company uses that password system for all their clients. That way, if they hire a new employee, they can tell the employee, "Here's a list of 50 companies that need to have their networks taken care of. Go ahead and run out there and take care of them. By the way, the domain administrator password is the first word of their company name."

I later asked the CEO, "How did you know that was a good outsource company to use?" He proceeded to pull out the phone book and opened to the IT section. "See," he said, pointing to their listing. "They have a half-page ad."

Fortunately, he doesn't use them anymore, and he doesn't judge IT companies by the size of their phone book ad anymore either.

Realize, too, that not all outsource providers are like the company in this example. I'm simply showing you the kinds of things you need to be aware of.

Okay, so now let's look at the pros.

The biggest pro of using an outsource IT provider is the level of expertise you can get. For example, how would you feel if you walked into the hospital and the receptionist said to you, "Good morning. We'd like to introduce you to Dr. Smith. He's our resident cardiologist. He's also our resident brain surgeon, our resident neurologist, our resident OB/GYN doctor, our resident…" If you were to hear that, would you think this doctor is really qualified in anything? No way!

Yet, in IT, it used to be that one person could be an expert in everything IT related. But because IT has expanded so much over the years, that's not so anymore. Even so, many IT professionals still think it's their responsibility to do everything in the IT department. Often, this can cause problems. That's when you need to bring in outside help. Bring in someone who is an expert in what you need done.

Additionally, outsourced IT professionals see many different businesses and often recognize problems early on, before they have a chance to damage your organization. Also consider that when you outsource your IT needs, you don't have to send people to expensive schools and long training programs so they can learn how to configure some device that will only need to be configured once. Even better, some IT outsource firms have alliances with vendors that can get you special pricing on hardware and software. Finally, should your own IT professionals move on or become ill, it would be nice to have a solid outsourced IT firm to fall back on during emergencies.

Therefore, be sure you support your IT professional, especially if he or she says to you, "We're getting ready to install the latest version of Exchange. It'd be really nice to have someone else come in and set up Exchange." So make it okay for your IT professionals to bring someone else in if they want to. That's when you're using IT outsource providers in the most effective way. You're relying on the specific expertise of someone to help your company get over a hump or take care of a challenge.

Action Item: Even if you have an IT staff, investigate some IT outsource firms. Call them and meet with them to discover how they can assist you with your IT needs.

CHAPTER 7

Securinoia

People often say to me, "I don't care how many security reviews a company gets. You can come in and look at a system and make recommendations. You can install all the updates and fixes and patches available. But a month later, something is going to change and you'll be vulnerable again. So at some point you just have to accept the fact that stuff happens and you can't worry about every little thing."

And I totally agree. In fact, there's something in the IT industry known as securinoia. It's when someone constantly worries that they're going to get hacked.

As in anything in life, extremes in IT security are not good. You don't want to be at the point where you say, "Gee, if someone wants my information, they're going to find a way to get it, so why bother with security."

At the other end of the spectrum, you don't want to be at the point where you say, "Oh my gosh. Did I hear a bit go by? Was that a friendly bit or a bad bit?" You don't want to be at either end of the spectrum. You need to be in between, as that's where it's healthy. To do so, you simply need to use best practices.

Think of it this way: I would venture a guess that if I showed up at your business at midnight on Friday night, the doors would be locked. Why do you lock those doors? Well, you know good and well that someone could break into your company. But if they wanted to, they could get past those locked doors, couldn't they? Couldn't they bring a bulldozer and plow right through your front door? So why bother locking the doors? Because the bulldozer scenario is relatively far-fetched.

Similarly, you likely don't hire someone to come by every hour on the hour when you're closed to make sure the doors are locked. And if you do, then I'd hope you are as careful with your IT security!

With that said, though, you probably don't have a flimsy lock on your door. I imagine you have something reliable and industrial, not a little bedroom door lock like you have in your house.

You also probably know who is supposed to lock the door at night. You don't just call over your shoulder as you leave each evening, "Hey…last one out lock the door."

The point is that you strike a balance when it comes to physically locking your company's doors at night. The same kind of balance needs to apply to your internet security. So don't get paranoid about everything I'm telling you, but don't blow it all off either. Get to a spot that's good for you and your company's needs. Then you'll sleep better at night and have fewer things to worry about.

Action Item: *Assess your own needs in terms of security. Are they realistic? Or are they too loose or too tight?*

CHAPTER 8

Identity Theft

In the past five years, over thirty-three million people have had their identity stolen. And according to *USA Today*, the average victim loses over $92,000 and six hundred work hours due to identity theft. These facts don't even take into account the emotional turmoil many victims endure.

Realize that your most valuable possession is not your house, your car, your business, or your art collection. Your most valuable possession is what makes you—your identity. What would happen if someone stole it?

While many people believe that identity theft is nothing more than someone stealing your credit cards and racking up charges, the fact is that identity theft has many forms and can do much more damage than simply ruin your credit. As an identity theft victim, you could end up in serious trouble with the IRS or even in jail.

The people I have spoken to who have been victims of identity theft tell me that life is miserable for a while. You need to go to an all cash basis as you're trying to get your records straight. You can't use credit cards, if the thief stole your DMV record you may not be allowed a driver's license, and you may find out you owe a lot of money to the IRS due to someone else working under your social security number and not paying taxes on the income.

Why does identity theft happen? Well, here is my understanding of the mind of an identity thief. Think of them as people who are addicted to drugs and need their next fix. Many of them honestly believe that they may not live if they don't get their next score, because they're addicted to purchasing things under someone else's name, just like a drug addict. And, some of the identity thieves or their customers are drug addicts, and that is where the money goes.

So they'll get people's identities, apply for credit cards in those names, and they'll get one of those credit cards where you get a certain amount of money right up front. They'll use that money, and when it runs out, they just toss the card and go on to the next one.

The current research shows that these thieves can purchase someone's identity anywhere from around $16 to about $70. Then, in theory, the novice thieves are going to get $700 worth of transactions from that identity until they have to move on to the next one. The professional identity thieves can get hundreds of thousands of dollars before someone gets wise to them.

Now, from a business standpoint, you have some responsibility for stopping identity theft. On June 1, 2005, the FTC's rule on the proper storage and disposal of certain "consumer information" went into effect. This rule was issued by the

FTC as part of its jurisdiction under the Fair And Accurate Credit Transactions Act or FACTA.

The law requires that any business that maintains or otherwise possesses consumer information, or any compilation of consumer information derived from consumer reports for a business purpose must properly store and dispose of such information or compilation. The new rule is supposed to cut down on the incidences of identity theft by restricting the ability of thieves to go "dumpster diving" for valuable consumer information contained in discarded business records.

Why should your business care about complying with the FACTA rules? Well, FACTA rules apply to any business that directly or indirectly has or uses consumer information, regardless of the business' size or number of employees. Because FACTA can apply to every business, every business should want to keep its records safe and dispose of them properly. Just to add an extra incentive to ensure compliance, FACTA provides for a range of civil liabilities and penalties for noncompliance.

For example, a business that fails to comply with the FACTA rules can be liable for actual damages in a civil lawsuit brought by anyone whose identity is stolen as a result. And, for those businesses that love the thought of being a defendant in a class action lawsuit, FACTA allows class action lawsuits to be filed too. So this is one ruling you don't want to mess with and just another reason why you need to be sure your IT system is secure.

Action Item: Take inventory of all personal data stored on your network. Do you keep names, addresses, birthdates, social security numbers, credit card numbers, bank information, medical records, personal history, or any other sensitive data?

CHAPTER 9

Encrypted Data

So as you can see, data security is a big issue for companies, and no one is untouchable. Even worse, the attacks on companies' IT systems aren't diminishing. In February 2007, 2.2 million active duty personnel records were compromised, and unfortunately, many of them were not encrypted.

What's encryption? It's when the data is scrambled in such a way that no one can read it. With all that's happening in the world today, you'd think everyone would encrypt their data, especially on laptops, hard drives, memory sticks, and other devices that are easily carried out of the office, but they don't.

I do security reviews for companies all the time, and I can't think of a single company that I've been to that didn't have at least one laptop out in the field with unencrypted data. And in fact, none of the companies I've worked with yet use something called full-disk encryption on every single one of their laptop systems.

When it comes to data encryption, some people use the encryption tool built into their word processing program. That's a good start, but it's not nearly enough. When I travel I sometimes bring my "penetration testing" laptop with me if I'll need it on that trip. On that laptop I have special "hacker tools." One of the things I like to do during my presentations to business executives is set a password in my word processing program and then save a file.

Now everyone in the audience believes that data is encrypted, and it is, but only at the bare minimum. I then show the audience how easy it is to crack the encryption code.

The first thing I show them is how they can right click on the file, and then click on the summary tab. By doing this, you can read the first line of the file—even though the file is encrypted. So if you have an employee who you suspect may be up to no good, you can right click on their files, choose the summary tab, and read the first line of their files. Who knows…maybe you'll see one that has a first line of, "This is how I'm going to sell our information to our competitors," or something similar that would implicate the employee.

Then I run a password tool program on the computer—something any good hacker has in his or her arsenal—and usually by the first meeting break, the password program has cracked the code and all the encrypted data is available for full viewing.

At that, most executives are amazed. "Wow. I didn't know you can do that," is all they're able to say.

On top of that, have you ever had your computer shut down abnormally, while you were in the middle of working in your word processing program, and when the computer rebooted and you tried to re-open your work, your word processing program displayed the file you were just working on with a message that it automatically saved a copy of your work?

That's an unencrypted copy—even if the original version of the file was encrypted. The danger here is that, if your word processing program saves unencrypted files as "backup copies" while you are working on the file, even though the word processing program deletes the files when you close out normally, the "deleted" unencrypted backup copies aren't really deleted until they are written over. A malicious hacker could potentially use a data remembrance tool to read those "we thought they were deleted" unencrypted backup copies of your confidential information.

There's also something in most computer systems called a paging file. It's a way that the computer stores information about what you are working on "right then" even if you don't have enough "chip memory" installed in your computer to process multiple and/or large programs. This way your computer doesn't have to totally rely on just the chip memory you have installed. In other words, it sets aside part of the hard drive and pretends that it's chip memory too. If your confidential document gets copied to the paging file while you are editing the confidential file, then that information gets stored in that paging file in an unencrypted manner.

So even if you use the built in encryption feature of your word processing program, there are still all these copies of your files available. That's why you need what's called full-disk encryption. Quite simply, it encrypts everything on your drive.

Many people say they don't use full-disk encryption tools because they think it's expensive. Well, it's not expensive at all. I have full-disk encryption that came included for free with my laptop. Some people also believe that security is very difficult to configure. No. Enabling full-disk encryption only adds about forty-five seconds to your computer's setup once the IT professional knows the procedure. It's very easy.

Other people say, "Once you use full-disk encryption, it becomes almost impossible for the end user to use the computer." That was true at one point. But now, if I want to lock my laptop, all I have to do is use the Windows L key combination and the computer locks, or I can just set the computer to lock automatically if I walk away for very long. Then whenever I want to get back in, I can take any one of my ten fingers and swipe it across the fingerprint reader that is on the front of the laptop. Now I'm ready to go again and can access all the data on the system.

People also tell me that encryption is slow. It's not. I use my laptop to run large and involved programs all the time, so I need speed. And I have overkill encryption on my machine just to prove to audiences how fast it is. I have my data locked or encrypted three different ways, and it only needs to be encrypted once. This is to demonstrate the speed.

So in a nutshell, full disk encryption security is inexpensive, it's easy for the user, it's very important to have, and it's easy for your IT administrators, too. So it's time to be secure, and full-disk encryption is a great start to having some peace of mind.

Action Item: Investigate some full-disk encryption tools and make sure everyone in your office encrypts their data.

CHAPTER 10

Cell Phone Security

When it comes to IT security, our computers aren't the only thing vulnerable. Almost everyone these days has a cell phone, and a cell phone can be hacked too.

One way to infect someone's cell phone is with a malicious program called FlexiSPY. Here's how it works. Let's say that Dave, our company president, wants to follow up a little bit on one of his senior managers, Greg, and find out what he's up to. Dave would simply go to Greg sometime and say, "Greg, do you mind if I borrow your mobile phone? Mine's not working and I want to check in with my family." And Greg says, "Sure, no problem."

So Dave takes his phone. Now Dave has already been to FlexiSPY, and they've already given him the instructions of how to infect Greg's phone with a little virus by simply visiting a web site URL. So Dave does that. He acts like he's dialing the number, and then just to make it look good, he says into the phone, "Yeah, hi. I was just checking in. Is everything okay? Oh yeah, Greg loaned me his phone. He's a great guy. Okay. I'll talk to you later. Bye." Then Dave hands Greg his phone back.

Meanwhile, Greg thinks everything is just dandy. He loaned his boss his phone and he's a good guy. But now, any phone calls that Greg places or receives, Dave is going to get a report of who the other party is, what their phone number is, and how long they were on the phone. All that information is available to Dave for just $49.95.

Now, if Dave decided to splurge and spend $149.95, he can remotely activate the microphone on Greg's phone and actually listen in on Greg's activities any time Greg's phone is turned on. So if Greg is at home tonight with his family, Dave could listen to their conversation at the dinner table. If Greg is in a closed meeting, Dave could listen to the closed meeting. Essentially, Dave could hear anything going on in Greg's life, as long as his phone is turned on.

The CIA knows what a serious danger this technology is. In fact, the CIA is very concerned that this spying technology might get on the cell phones of some of the Chief Justices of the Supreme Court or other high-ranking government officials. If that were to happen, it would really undermine the security of the United States of America.

Therefore, never hand your phone to anyone. If someone asks me to borrow my cell phone, I say, "Sure. But I'm going to dial your number, and I'm going to stand two inches from your face the entire time you have the conversation."

At that, the person who asked to borrow my cell phone usually replies, "Never mind."

If you have recently handed someone your cell phone to use and are wondering if some sort of spying device is on your phone, you could have your IT professional examine the phone. Or, if your phone is getting out of date anyway, now might be a good time to trade in your phone for a new one. You can keep the same phone number, since the virus affects the phone itself and not the phone number.

If you ever look at your phone and see the screen says that the phone is "connected" or "in use" when you didn't place a call or answer a call, then this may indicate that you have some sort of phone spyware on it. Unfortunately, most people don't look at their phone when they're not using it. They just leave it in their belt clip, purse, pocket, in a desk drawer, or on a table.

You would also see tell-tale signs of someone spying on your calls on your phone bill. But not everyone examines their bill, and some people never even see their bills if they use a bookkeeper to mind their finances.

If you have the right tools, you can figure out if something was loaded onto your phone. One company called Trust Digital makes a very nice central management tool to audit, manage, and protect all of your phones and PDA's in the enterprise.

A common theme you will notice in this book for protecting your network is the concept of "Central Management." What's that? Well, ask any IT professional, and they'll tell you that one of the worst things in our career is when we have to change something on all the company's computers. It doesn't matter if you have five computers, fifty computers, five hundred computers, or more, that's way too much work to visit each computer, phone, or PDA, individually. We want to be able to manage things centrally.

Today's organizations have PDAs, cell phones, Blackberries, etc. All of these devices also hold sensitive data. So what happens when one of your employees is traveling for business and accidentally leaves his mobile phone or PDA in a taxi? If you had a central management system in place, that employee would simply call the IT department and tell them what happened. Then someone in IT can make a few keystrokes on the keyboard and erase everything in that particular phone or PDA.

Now, everything on that phone gets securely erased. And when I say securely erased, that means inside that phone it's writing ones and zeros on the data card to actually erase information. Even data forensics can't get that data back anymore. It's just gone.

In the event that whoever rides in the taxi next finds the phone and somehow returns it to you, your IT department can make a few more keystrokes on the keyboard and restore all the data. That sure beats having to go through a four-hour process of reloading everything.

So don't overlook your cell phone and PDA when it comes to data security. There are tools out there that will help you—use them.

Action Item: Treat your cell phone like you treat your toothbrush. Never let anyone use it.

CHAPTER 11

Network Security

S o far we've talked about security on individual computers and cell phones, let's move a little larger in scope now and address securing your entire network.

In a typical office you have however many individual computers that are all hooked to the company's network. Each computer has its own programs and data. The question is, if the network is protected, does that mean that all the computers that are "connected to the network" are also protected?

The answer is yes…and no. And, in some cases, connecting an infected computer to the network can infect the entire network!

Most companies have a firewall between the network and the Internet. The firewall's job, in the simplest terms, is to let the good things through and block the bad stuff. Some people think, "Connecting to a network that is protected by a firewall is all I need to be sure my computer is protected," which certainly makes sense. But it's a bit like living in a gated community where there's a guard. Even though you have security in your community provided by the guard at the gate, chances are you still lock your doors to your home. Think of your network protection in the same way.

For example, let's say one of your employees, Lucy, goes off on a business trip and stays at one of the national hotel chains that offers free wireless Internet. So Lucy works hard while on her trip, staying connected to the Internet so she can be even more productive.

But while she's online at the hotel, her computer gets infected. When Lucy comes back to the office and plugs in her computer into the network, guess what happens. The infection on Lucy's computer starts looking for ways to replicate itself on other machines. If all the individual computers aren't protected, Lucy's virus is going to get on every computer inside the network.

Have you ever had a virus infect your company and someone say to you, "Wow. I don't understand how that got through our firewall." When that happens, there is a good chance that some person brought the virus in from the outside by physically carrying a laptop or some form of removable media into the office "right past the firewall." This allowed the infection to go "around" instead of "through" the firewall.

That's why you need to secure your the individual workstations as well as the network. And whether you have three computers or three hundred, you need to have everyone on a domain model, not workgroup model, with a dedicated server. That will give you a central management point so you can take care of all the machines automatically.

Also realize that your company's computer network is only as strong as its weakest link. Often I hear in companies that the CEO won't let anyone from IT touch his or her computer. But if all the other computers in the network are up to date except the CEO's, your company is still vulnerable. So you have to make sure everyone's computer, even the CEO's, is protected.

Realize that much of the information in the remaining chapters will give you more details on various aspects of network security and what you can do. For now, I simply want you to understand the importance of securing the network in addition to individual workstations, and visa versa.

So if your IT professional says they want to make your computer safe, let them. That's what they get paid to do.

Action Item: Ask your IT professionals if there are any computers in the organization they are "reluctant to touch" with patches, anti-virus, or any other security procedures and tools. If so, are they reluctant because of who the user of the computer is, or because they fear the system is unstable and don't want to change anything since the computer might not work anymore, or are there other reasons?

CHAPTER 12

Who Are the Hackers?

As you can see, just about everything is vulnerable to hackers. At this point, many people wonder, "Who are these hackers? And why do they hack?"

Here's a real-life scenario of a typical hacker. A company in the Midwest announced to one of their IT professionals that they were "freeing up his future" (in other words, they fired him). Well, this person didn't react well to the situation. So he chose to hack back into the company's system and he found the company Christmas card. On the card was a Christmas tree, and on the tree were colored balls with frost. The fired IT professional took the frost on one of the balls and changed it to be in the shape of a middle finger in a rude gesture.

Well, the company didn't notice this slight alteration, and they printed up thousands of Christmas cards and sent them to all of their customers and vendors.

A few days later, the phone calls and the e-mails started coming in.

The CEO asked me what he should do.

I said, "Send him a thank you card for not doing more damage than that. It could have been a lot worse. And block his access to the network!"

In some companies, those IT professionals who have their future freed up are a bit more malicious. They hack into their former company's computers and delete sensitive and important data that the company can't function without.

So the bottom line is that you have to prevent hacking from happening.

In addition to former employees seeking revenge, people hack for adventure (the thrill of the crime), curiosity ("I wonder how well protected the sensitive data at ABC company is"), and for ego ("I bet I can beat any system"). Then there are what the FBI calls "script kiddies." That's when teenagers (and sometimes pre-teens) play around with hacking tools other people have written.

Unfortunately, there's big profit in hacking. According to Ted Bridis, an Associated Press writer who recently wrote a news story on identity thieves selling television character Herman Munster's identity, "A consumer's financial details can be worth $4 and $40 among online thieves, who can use the information to open fraudulent credit accounts." Other sources, such as InfoWatch.com, a company that specializes in protecting the most valuable resource any company has—its confidential information—say that some identity thieves make even more. For example, they claim that for $40 you can purchase an account with an open credit limit of $3,000 and over, and for $400 you can purchase an account with an open credit limit of $31,000. The thieves can even provide specific information such as signatures, social security numbers, date of birth, and e-mail address. Of course, identities with these extra bits of information are more expensive.

So, theoretically, the person who hacked UCLA and got those 800,000 names made about $32 million in a little over an hour or however long it took them to hack the system, all while sitting at home in their jammies. That's pretty good income—$32 million a day for working in your jammies.

Realize, too, that if someone wants to hack into Fred's computers, they aren't going to hack straight into Fred's machine. They're going to go through Brock's computer, which will lead them to Peter's network, which will put them through Mary's network, which will put them through Max's computer, which will then get them to Fred's computer. So if Fred spends money hiring a data forensics specialist to go back and track all this down, they're going to show up on Max's door and say, "Someone in your company hacked us and we have to find out who." Then they spend a lot of money and time only to find out that the problem didn't originate at Max's company. If they invest even more time and money, they'll trace back to Mary's network, and so on.

Hackers love to work like that. There are even tools on the Internet now that let them hide so that they can do the malicious behavior and be totally anonymous as they do it. As a result, tracking hackers is more difficult now than ever before. If you have time and are interested, you may want to investigate TOR, The Onionskin Router, for an example of how this evasion can be performed.

Some hackers imbed malicious tools in web sites. These are scripts you can install on your web page, and then try to attract people to your web page. If the visitor's computer is not well protected, then your scripts would infect their computer and allow you to do things, such as monitor their activity, capture their credit card numbers, and inject viruses on their computer. You could also use the other person's computer for malicious purposes, maybe to send out spam or to store things on their computer that you don't want to store on your computer.

How bad can it get for someone whose computer is hacked? Here's a real example. On December 7, 2006, a lady in Denver woke up one morning to four sheriffs pounding on her door. When she answered the door, the sheriff's weapons were drawn, and they had a search warrant. Only thing is… this woman didn't do anything illegal.

As it turns out, hackers had gotten into her computer and were using her computer to make fraudulent credit card charges. The woman said that she had a personal firewall installed on her computer, but she had turned it off because it slowed her computer down too much. I guess she thought it was much better to have a faster computer than a secure one.

I wish I could say that her story is unique, but it's not.

One time a company on the East Coast was hacked, and they had me track down the location of the hacker. The results came up Thailand. The CEO made the comment, "Wow. Isn't it amazing someone that far away could hack in?" I could tell he "didn't get it." Think about his statement. How far away is Thailand on the Internet? The whole world is basically in our own shirt pocket.

We try to "stay out of bad neighborhoods" when we travel, choose where to live, and choose where to put our businesses. Realize that once we connect to the Internet, we are in all neighborhoods—good and bad—at once.

So realize that hackers can be anyone: the ex-employee, the bored teenager, or the hard-core thief. There's no one single profile of who a hacker is or why he or she hacks. The best you can do is arm yourself with the proper tools to protect yourself from these people. And that precisely what the remainder of this book will show you.

Action Item: Ask IT about your employees. Are the HR employees the only ones who can see employee records? Are there any left over user accounts on your network for employees who are no longer with the company?

CHAPTER 13

Update and Patch Your Operating System and Applications

To keep your computers and network safe, you need to regularly update your operating system and your applications. Since most companies use Microsoft operating systems, let's focus our discussion there first.

Microsoft, as we're all aware, is not perfect (but then again, few companies or products are). However, Microsoft is very good about releasing patches to fix flaws and vulnerabilities as they are discovered.

I know...I know....you may have installed a patch a few years ago and then your system didn't work right after that. Granted, in the past some patches created problems, but that was *in the past*. These days Microsoft invests tremendous effort into making sure the patches are solid before being released. Additionally, we'll cover some other strategies to keep yourself from falling prey in the unlikely event there is a problem with a patch. So please don't think, "If it ain't broke, don't fix it." You need to install patches to keep your system safe.

For example, a while back when Windows 2000 was the latest and greatest operating system, Microsoft released a high priority patch and even warned consumers that if you don't install this patch, hackers could easily crash your system. Well, guess who didn't apply their patches? CNN and The New York Times. And yes, hackers got in and crashed their systems.

How much did Microsoft charge for that patch these companies neglected to install? Not a penny. Patches are free. This illustrates how inexpensive it can be to keep your system more secure.

The whole concept of patches can be complex. So let's go over some of the important aspects of patches.

First, I encourage everyone to go to www.microsoft.com. On the right-hand side of the web page you'll see the words "Security and Updates." Click it. At the new screen you'll be taken to, click "Microsoft Update." This is different than going to Windows Update. Microsoft Update is the newer, better flavor of the old Windows Update.

At the window you're now on, choose "Express." Now your computer will scan itself and will tell you what patches are needed on your machine. The results will be split into categories such as "High Priority," "Software Optional," and "Hardware Optional" updates.

The high priority patches (that is, the ones that appear at the top of your results screen) are the only ones you need to be concerned with at this point. I hope that your results say that you don't need any high priority patches, indicating that your IT department is keeping your computer up to date. However, when I visit companies to perform security reviews, it is rare that all the systems are current with their high priority updates.

If your results come back that you need many high priority patches, then your IT department has some explaining to do.

The high priority updates are very important, because they either fix a security problem that Microsoft knows about or they fix something else important that's broken in Windows, which could cause your system to malfunction. So high priority patches are the ones you need.

I've seen many companies run Microsoft Update and get some long laundry lists of high priority patches. As a typical example, a company I visited in 2007 had the following results:

- One employee's computer needed six patches—the oldest outstanding one going back to May 13th 2005.

- Another employee's computer needed fourteen patches—the oldest outstanding one going back to September 2nd 2004.

- The SQL server needed fourteen patches—the oldest outstanding one going back to May of 2006.

- Their terminal server needed fourteen patches—the oldest outstanding one going back to November 2005.

- Their Exchange server hadn't been patched since November 2005.

- They had two other servers that had *never* been patched.

This is a company that's using a tool I'm going to cover in Chapter Fifteen called WSUS. It's an important tool, but their IT professional wasn't using it correctly. This company is a good example of what you discover sometimes when you have someone else come in and look at your system. I was able to show the grateful IT professional what he needed and the systems are up to date now.

Not having your computers properly updated and patched can cause big problems for you, so I'm going to give you the strategy for these updates.

1. High priority updates: Get them…right away.

2. Software Optional updates: These are optional and are totally up to you. In your software update list you'll see updates for things like Windows Media Player. If you don't care about the particular software program or don't use it, then don't bother.

3. Hardware Optional updates: Never install these on your system unless your IT professional tells you to.

Because of the architecture of the Windows operating system, the Hardware Optional updates are the ones that are most likely to crash your system and cause the dreaded B.S.O.D. (blue screen of death) error. If your Hardware Optional update list says that there's a new HP driver and your HP printer doesn't have a problem, then don't worry about the update. If your printer does have a problem, go to HP to get your driver.

After you install the priority updates, you need to scan for updates again. Why? Sometimes the updates need updating. So yes, you may have to update your updates.

We will talk about the best way to monitor and apply Microsoft patches in the chapter about WSUS.

Finally, make sure you're using recent operating systems only. Operating systems like NT, ME, SE, 98, and so on are okay if they control a big laser cutter out in the warehouse, for example, or some type of machinery. But please get computers with those old operating systems off your network.

Those computers have vulnerabilities that Microsoft no longer makes patches for. Therefore, unplug them from the network, fill the Ethernet card with epoxy or something so people can't plug in the cable anymore. Use those computers for specific functions if you have to, but not on the network.

If you need to get information over to one of those machines, copy the information onto a CD or a memory stick and take it there using what we refer to as "Sneaker Net." (By the way, when you physically carry files from one computer to another using a CD or a memory stick, that is called "Sneaker-Net.") If you're in a situation where you need the older machines connected to your network, then there are other alternatives that sometimes work, such as running the older operating system in a virtual machine hosted on secure machine using a current operating system and a tool such as VMWare from www.vmware.com. I realize that you don't want to interrupt your users' ability to get their work done, yet at the same time, you have to make sure you're secure.

I want to emphasize that as you apply patches to your operating system, also make patches to your applications. Why is this important? Think of it this way: If you lock your doors, the thieves may try to come in through the windows. In other words, if the hackers can't get in through the Operating System vulnerabilities, then they will attempt to exploit your applications. That's why these need to be patched as well.

As you update, pay attention to whether something is a feature update or a security update. Feature updates simply add new functionality to a program. So it doesn't matter whether you install feature updates or not. What I want you to be concerned with are the security updates and patches. Without the proper security patches on your applications, your computer is vulnerable to a hacker attack.

As with the operating system updates, it is better for the application updates to be centrally managed. If your primary applications are from Microsoft, such as Microsoft Office for example, then the aforementioned Microsoft Update tool and the WSUS tool that is in a later chapter will help you patch the Microsoft applications as well. If you rely on non-Microsoft applications then you may choose to use a tool such as www.patchlink.com to manage your patches.

PatchLink will patch your applications and your Operating System as well for a nominal fee per user per year.

Realize that you don't have to pick one or the other: usability or security. These days, you can have both in almost all circumstances. Good IT professionals know that sometimes the solution will evade you like the last move of a chess game, and the victory is worth the effort invested to find the solution. And, in rare unhappy circumstances, we just have to rely on our other layers of security to keep the older operating systems secure for a period of time until they can be upgraded.

Action Item: Go to Microsoft Update right now and scan your computer for the needed patches.

CHAPTER 14

Update Your Firmware

In addition to updating your operating system and your programs, you also need to update your firmware.

Firmware is what we call the programs that run inside your appliances, such as the router and your wireless access point. These are appliances we have on our network that don't really look like a computer on the outside, but they do have a computer running inside.

The government learned about updating firmware the hard way. A U.S. military installation's laboratory and NASA both got hit, and the way they got hit was through an exploit in their Cisco firewall.

This is not to say that Cisco firewalls are bad. Think about it. There's one Cisco and thousands of hackers; the hackers are finding ways into Cisco all the time.

So how does Cisco respond to that? What do you suppose they do?

Cisco goes to great lengths to find out about fixes they need to release, and they do release patches regularly on time.

And how much does the patch cost?

Not a cent. You simply have to apply it.

Unfortunately, in many cases, company IT departments are going to apply firmware patches first thing tomorrow... forever. And that's exactly what happened at the U.S. military and at NASA. In this particular case, the focus of the investigation was on a youth—a pre-teen actually. So some little kid got into the U.S. military and NASA. It sounds like a joke, but it's the truth.

The FBI refers to these kids as script kiddies, because they find the tools on the Internet that adults have written, and then the kids use them because they're bored and don't have much self-restraint.

But if someone gets into your network and destroys a bunch of your data or causes other problems in your system, it doesn't matter if it's a kid or an adult. It still causes the same amount of problems.

Your IT professionals will consult the documentation that came with your appliances to discover how to find and apply updates. This process usually involves going to the appliance manufacturer's web site, navigating to the "support" and then "downloads" to find the current patches. Next, download all security patches, but not necessarily feature patches. Then backup the current configuration of the appliance in a method that will allow a simple restoration process in the event of a problem with the new patches. The whole process will be documented in the instructions and generally finishes here with the actual installation of the new firmware. Sometimes the backed up configuration will need to be restored as well.

Action Item: Make a list of all the firmware on your system and take the steps to get any needed patches.

CHAPTER 15

WSUS

WSUS stands for Windows Server Update Services. It's a wonderful tool that I encourage you to get in your company. This tool has many features, and three of the most notable are addressed in this chapter.

First, no matter how many computers you have on your corporate network, WSUS downloads all your updates just once to one of your machines. So if you have three hundred computers in your company, only one computer has to get the updates rather than all three hundred. This greatly reduces the necessary bandwidth needed to download updates, freeing up your Internet connection to handle other traffic.

Second, even though it is unlikely that an update will cause a problem on your systems, you can also deploy the updates to your computers in stages.

For example, you can instruct WSUS to deploy the updates first to just one computer. You then run that machine and make sure everything still works the way it's supposed to. If that computer is okay, then the IT department rolls the updates out to maybe five or six more machines. If all of those computers are okay, then you might put the update on fifty machines. If they're all skill okay, then you'd put the updates on 150 machines. If everything is still working properly, then you can update all the remaining machines.

Why bother doing the updates in stages like that?

Well, perhaps a particular update won't run well on your system. You certainly don't want to run the risk of deploying the update to every computer in your company and then shut down all 300 computers. As I mentioned earlier, these days the patches and updates are almost always okay. But you still don't want to take that risk. You don't want to walk in Wednesday morning and learn that nobody can use their computer. That would be just as bad as a hacker attack and cause the same amount of damage. So you want to deploy updates in stages.

Third, the best part of WSUS, which makes it worth much more money than it costs, is the central management and monitoring functionality WSUS provides.

Later in this book we will discuss how important it is to give your IT professionals ten minutes every morning to perform a "ten-minute daily check." If you outsource your IT, assign someone in your office to perform this daily check or have your outsourced IT professionals log in remotely to perform the daily check. One of the parts of the daily check is to look at the WSUS screen that shows which computers need updates. This is much better than your IT professional having to run around and look at every computer every day and/or not knowing which computers need updating. If there are any computers that need high priority updates, your IT professional can install the updates. Thanks to the central management provided by WSUS, no one has to run to each computer every day to check for updates, nor do you have to rely on the users to check their own computers, which never works anyway.

Guess how much this WSUS costs per seat on your network? Many applications are sold on a "per seat" basis where you pay based on the number of computers you will be using.

Well, believe it or not, Microsoft provides WSUS totally free of charge. That's something all of us could afford for sure.

So the bottom line is, if your IT department is not using WSUS, please encourage them to do so. And if you find yourself saying, "Our IT guy has have never set up WSUS before and he's busy with everything else," then find a Microsoft Certified Systems Engineer (MCSE) you trust that you can outsource to. Let that person set up the WSUS for you. Realize too, that thanks to the wonders of remote access, MCSE doesn't even have to physically come to your office if you can provide them remote access into your network.

Remember that if you have non-Microsoft applications like AutoCAD and other applications that you have to manually visit every computer to update, then consider using a company such as PatchLink. For $15 per user per year plus around $1600 for the server component, (as of this publication date) PatchLink keeps everything updated on your system, much like WSUS does, except PatchLink does all programs, not just Microsoft. So now your IT professionals don't have to use WSUS. They just use PatchLink, and it covers everything, Microsoft and non-Microsoft.

> **Action Item: Check to see if your IT department is using WSUS. If not, get it today.**

CHAPTER 16

Patch Tuesday and Hacker Wednesday

Microsoft releases patches generally once a month, on what's called "Patch Tuesday," which is the second Tuesday of the month. Why only once a month? Because it makes IT's job easier. Patches used to be released at multiple random times during each month, which was frustrating due to the interruption of all IT professionals' schedules. Now, Microsoft strives to release patches one day a month so IT professionals can plan ahead. They can schedule themselves accordingly so they're ready for the updates and prepared just in case there's a problem with an update.

The problem is that as soon as Microsoft invented Patch Tuesday, the hackers invented Hacker Wednesday to release their latest exploits. They know that it's going to be 30 days before Microsoft releases patches again. So the day after Patch Tuesday is the best day for hackers to get their tools out there.

Hacker Wednesday exploits illustrate something called a Zero Day Attack, meaning the hacker puts something bad out there, and it does as much damage as it can before Microsoft makes the patch for it, or before your anti-virus program figures out the exploit is a virus. In the world of hackers, releasing a Zero Day Attack is a useful strategy.

Now, if the hackers release an exploit that is so serious that Microsoft feels the problem will do a lot damage, they will release a security patch as soon as the patch is tested and proven. Microsoft won't make you wait until the next patch Tuesday.

Microsoft invests a great deal of energy into making sure the patch to fix the vulnerability won't break anything else on the system. Microsoft learned the hard way years ago that if their patches break other things in your network, you will be reluctant to apply Microsoft patches from then on. They've managed to rebuild their reputation for providing reliable patches, at least at the workstation level, and they plan to keep doing a good job of testing before releasing from now on.

As a result of Microsoft's delayed release of patches, you will sometimes find third parties who release a "fix" before Microsoft releases the fix. Take the dangerous step of using a third party patch at your own risk, realizing the "third party" may or may not have tested their patches thoroughly.

Action Item: Make sure your IT professionals have the time and resources they need every Patch Tuesday so they can do their jobs effectively.

CHAPTER 17

Server Updates

When it comes to server updates, many companies don't rush to apply the patches to their servers immediately. They wait a little while because, if there happens to be a problem with a patch and it causes one or more services to malfunction on the server, then everyone connected to that server may be affected and will experience the loss of service.

To avoid having a bad server patch cause a problem on your entire network, one option is to wait a couple of weeks, maybe even four weeks, before you apply the patches to the servers.

Keep in mind two things. First, applying patches to workstations in a staged deployment using WSUS can happen right away since, even if there is a problem with the patch from Microsoft, few users will be affected if the staged deployment is done properly. Second, I want to reiterate that it is acceptable to wait two to four "weeks" before applying updates to servers, and not two to four "months" or "years."

An even better method is to test the patch in a test environment before deploying the patch to your production servers. One way to do this is to have one server that's not on the network and that is running a tool called VMWare. This server may be a recently retired server from your main network. With VMWare, you can configure the "test" server to be, virtually, the entire network inside one physical machine. Test the patch there first before releasing it into your organization's production servers.

Another great way to protect from problems with server updates is to keep your servers backed up with some form of image backup tool. Then, if the server crashes because of the patch (or any other reason for that matter), your IT team can more quickly repair the server by restoring the server to a state when it was working correctly. This is much better than having to rebuild the server's operating system from scratch and restore the data from a "normal, not an image" backup.

When your IT team is ready to apply the patch, they will make sure to have a current image backup of your system using a tool such as Symantec Live State Recovery or Acronis image backup for servers. This gives you the ability to, hopefully, be able to restore the server in one quick step if necessary. Then apply the patch. If the patch causes a problem, you just use Microsoft's option to roll back the patch, which usually works. If that doesn't work, you always restore your system using the image backup. Now you can go to work and figure out what you need to do to get the patch to work before you apply it again.

Whatever route you decide to take, remember that you can't wait years to install patches, as some companies do. Two to four weeks is the longest I recommend you go without the high priority patches. Anytime you're not patched, you are vulnerable.

Remember, it doesn't take long to have an attack, so keep your machines safe.

Action Item: Check with your IT to make sure regular updates are being done, not just on Patch Tuesday.

CHAPTER 18

Event Viewer Log Consolidation Tools

The more servers you have, the more difficult it is to track all the event viewer logs for errors without a log consolidating tool of some sort. Such a tool allows you to see alerts and other events that are important, without having to search through so many individual server logs.

Events to pay special attention to include, but are not limited to:

- Unusual logon/logoff events such as failed login attempts
- Any changes to system or executable files including DLLs, batch files, .ini files, etc. Monitor for changes to the file names as well
- Multiple access failures to files and other resources for specific files, folders, and/or users
- Gaps in the logs in case the logging service gets stopped by a hacker temporarily
- You will save even more time if your tool supports monitoring other logs as well
  - Open ports that you haven't approved

- Services you don't expect to have running, especially duplicate instances of other system services
- Router logs
- Firewall logs
- Anti-virus reports consolidated in to your event management solution
- Etc.
- Anything else out of the ordinary.

In some cases, organizations are required by law to monitor and archive event logs. Other organizations have benefited from the following log consolidation tools:

- Microsoft Operations Manager (MOM) www.microsoft.com/mom
- Argent Guardian www.argent.com

Less expensive but more limited options include:

- Dorian Event Log Management suite www.doriansoft.com
- Engagent Sentry II www.engagent.com
- GFI Events manager www.gfi.com/eventsmanager
- Prism Microsystems EventTracker www.eventlogmanager.com

Better tools have correlation processes that will help you by monitoring and analyzing the logs in real time to detect potential attacks that might go unnoticed otherwise. When a threat is detected, the process can send you an immediate alert so you can take appropriate action.

Action Item: Ensure that your IT professionals are using some sort of event viewer log consolidation tool so that they're using their using their time productively.

CHAPTER 19

User Beware

User Beware Item #1:

Have you ever booted up your machine and immediately got a little window on the bottom of your screen that says, "New updates are ready for your computer"?

That's a pop-up.

Beware, because pop-ups can be very dangerous. In fact, I would go so far as to recommend that you *never* click a pop-up unless you're 100% sure you know what it is. This is why you need tools protecting your computers, such as pop-up blockers, anti-virus, personal firewall, and anti-spyware software.

Pop-ups remind me of the time I was in Canada doing a security review. On my way home my flight landed in Chicago for a layover. When I got off the plane, I checked my voicemail and had a message from Citibank's fraud early warning department. They said I needed to call them back at a certain number to verify some charges on my card.

Now, I get calls like that all the time. But do you think I called back the number that they gave me? No way. I got out my Citibank card, looked at the back, and called the phone number printed there. Why? Because I know that's Citibank's number and not somebody just phishing for information.

Think about it. If you received a call from someone who said, "Hi. This is Mark from your bank. We need to verify some information. What's your social security number?", would you give the person your information? I sure hope not.

E-mails are very similar. For example, most security conscious banks have a policy that they will never send you an email with a link in it. In other words, they may say, "Go log into your account," but they will never say, "Click here to log into your account." So anytime you get an e-mail from your bank that says, "Click here to log in," know that it's probably not your bank. Just delete the message and move on. If you think it might be your bank, go to the bank's web site the way you normally do, by putting the bank's web site address in your browser, and do NOT click on the link in the e-mail message.

Even with all the scams out there, the good news is that you can protect your system.

First, don't ever click on a pop-up, even one from Microsoft Update, unless you're 100% sure you know it's really from that source. So if you have a personal firewall program and you open up Word, and your personal firewall pops up and says, "Word is trying to go to the Internet. Is that okay?" You have a fairly good idea that's legit, because you just opened Word and you got this message about Word.

But what if you were sitting there working in Word, and all of a sudden you get a message that says, "Excel is trying to go to the Internet. Is that okay?" But you're not even in Excel. In fact, you haven't used Excel in a month. In that case, the pop-up is very suspicious. So don't click on that pop-up in that case. Contact your IT team and have them check your computer to see how the pop-up made it past your security protection.

And realize that if the pop-up window has an X in the top right corner or even if it says "okay" or "cancel," hitting "cancel" or hitting the X is just as bad as saying "Hose me now." Because what they're trying to do is get you to interact with that box. When you interact, it can escalate the privileges of that process that's running on your system.

So again, no matter what pop-up comes across your screen, don't click it unless you both feel confident you know the source and you are aware of the risk you are taking.

User Beware Item #2:

Next, be wary of instant messenger; it's a vector for bad stuff to get into your computer, because it has something called peer-to-peer file sharing.

If you're using instant messaging just in your office, and your IT professionals have blocked instant messages from going out into cyberspace, then you don't have near the problem—at least as far as security goes. User productivity could be another issue depending on whether the messaging activity is important for your organization's bottom line.

The security problem is most prevalent when people are using instant messenger to go out into the world, which in many cases the communication is not solely for business needs. Sometimes they're just chatting with friends or with their kids. If IM is not important for your business, I recommend that you totally sever instant messenger at the firewall. Disable it so people can't even install it on their machines.

If instant messenger is crucial for your business, then you do have a few options. There are some Internet-based instant messaging tools, such as Meebo and eBuddy, where people actually go on the Internet and do their instant messaging there.

Another alternative is to have your IT professional set up IM to run in a virtual machine or a "sandbox" area on your computer so that, in theory, any infections won't be able to spread to the rest of the computer.

In any case, restrict IM to only those users who need access to Instant Messaging and block the other users. Most companies, though, can simply sever all IM capabilities and be okay.

Have you ever noticed that sometimes you can have a completely clean computer, and a teenager touches it, and in five minutes, through no intention of the teen, the computer is totally infected with everything? That's usually because of instant messenger. So it's quite a useful tool for infecting machines. My advice: Steer clear if it.

User Beware Item #3:

If you ever receive a blank e-mail with nothing attached and nothing in the body, and it's from someone you never heard of, you may be the recipient of an e-mail designed to harm your computer's security. There's an exploit running around in cyberspace right now, and what it does is it makes an entry in something in your computer called the hosts file, which is part of something called DNS.

Here's what DNS does: Whenever you type in a Uniform Resource Locator (URL) such as www.somename.com, your DNS redirects you to the actual website, which might be an address like 64.212.198.162. It's much more fun to say www.something.com than list out these numbers, and URLs are easier to remember as well.

Now, here's how this particular exploit works: Let's say you go to a bank's site, such as www.BigBank.com. If your host file has been modified by an exploit, you may think you're at Big Bank, but you're not. You've been redirected you to another site called "We're gonna hose you now," and they have mimicked the Big Bank login screen, which is something fairly easy to do if you're a web designer. Now you put in your username and password, and guess what… you just gave your username and password to hackers.

At this point, the hacker displays a pop-up window that says, "Error. You mistyped your password. Please try again." And then when you hit "okay" to retype your password, you get forwarded to the real Big Bank site. Now you put in your username and password again, and it works fine, and you forget anything ever happened. Meanwhile, you just gave your username and password to hackers.

Sound scary? It is. This prompted the federal government to mandate that by the end of 2006, every bank was required, for all their business accounts, to have some form of two-factor authentication, meaning more than just username and password.

Some banks responded to that by putting up a little picture they call a sight key. So every time you log in at your bank, you have to put in your username and password, and then they show you at least one picture that you're supposed to make sure is yours. Some banks show you three pictures, and you have to click on which one is yours.

That certainly makes it a lot harder for a very general attack to catch you.

Citibank chose to use a key fob—a little device they sent me to keep on my person. So anytime I'm getting ready to log into my Citibank business account, I push a little button on the key fob device and I get a six-digit number. At Citibank's web login screen I am required to enter my username, my password, and this six-digit number. Since the key fob is a physical device that you have, a hacker would have to steal it from you in order to gain access to your bank account.

The downside to a key fob goes back to user training. If you have someone at your company who decides to write the username and password on the back of their device, and then leave that device in their desk drawer, they're just asking for trouble.

Another thing banks may do is send you what they often refer to as a "bingo card," which means a sheet of paper that has alphanumeric codes arranged in rows and columns on it. Then when you put in your username and password, the bank's web site will say something like, "Please enter what is at Column C, Row 7." And you have to type in the code there. Then the bank knows it's you, because everyone has a different bingo card.

Another form of two factor authentication is called out-of-band signaling. That means when you enter your username and password, the bank sends a text message to your cell phone, PDA, pager, or other wireless device that displays a code you need to enter. So that way, a thief would have to know your username, password, and have your mobile phone or other wireless device.

As you can see, there are a lot of different strategies to two-factor authentication.

So from this day forward, be very careful when you're putting in your password at your bank. And if you get an error message when you know you typed the correct information, log into your bank on the second time and change your password immediately.

Action Item: Bring up these exploits in your next staff meeting. Consider having security awareness training for all of your employees.

CHAPTER 20

Anti-Virus Programs

Now we're going to move on to a topic everyone loves: Anti-virus programs. In fact, whenever I do a presentation, people always ask me, "What's the best virus utility program to use?"

That's a great question. And to be honest, for business use, I'm thrilled with just about all of them.

When I am performing vital systems reviews at client's offices, the most popular anti-virus package is the Norton/Symantec Anti-Virus Corporate Edition. The only problem I've seen with this tool is that because it is so popular, hackers have created viruses designed specifically to disable this anti-virus tool. Still, it is a very effective and valuable tool. Norton/Symantec is constantly combating the attacks against their products and, as long as you are current with updates, your system will normally be very secure.

Other companies that aren't quite as popular yet, but are equally good choices, include Trend Micro, Computer Associates, and many others. The good thing is that fewer targeted Trend Micro and Computer Associates attacks occur. So if you do get a virus that's designed to disable

Norton, for example, and you have Trend Micro installed, you hopefully won't be affected.

One of the most important aspects to evaluate is the effectiveness of the central monitoring console for your anti-virus solution. You want to be able to look at one screen to know the status of every computer on your network at that time. This process needs to become part of the ten minute daily check performed by one of your IT professionals or someone at your office. In one quick glance, it should be easy to see that every single one of your computers was scanned the night before, was clean of viruses, has the latest anti-virus signature file, and has the latest release of the anti-virus software. This way, problems can be fixed quickly, sometimes even before other symptoms show up.

It helps to check your computers with an online anti-virus tool occasionally from a company other than the manufacturer of your network anti-virus software. For example, if you have Symantec and think a virus may have disabled it on a specific computer, one way to see if viruses are present on the computer is to go to www.trendmicro.com. They have a free online scanning tool called House Call. Simply run House Call and see if it finds any viruses.

Now, if you can't get to Trend Micro or any other anti-virus site, you likely have a virus that's blocking you from getting the help you need. Hackers are getting more and more clever every day. It used to be that if you had a virus on your computer, you could buy anti-virus software and clean the virus off. But that's no longer the case. Sometimes you have to take the computer and completely wipe it and reinstall from scratch these days.

So if you cannot access any of the web sites you need to rid your computer of viruses, get some IT help immediately.

Action Item: Make sure you have some sort of centrally managed anti-virus running on all your computers. If you don't, install one today.

CHAPTER 21

Anti-Spyware Tools

S ome people don't realize that spyware got its start with adware. Adware is when you go on the Internet to look for a new car, and the next day you have 600 e-mails about where you can buy a new car. Some people might think to themselves, "Wow, what a coincidence!" But it's really adware at work.

As adware evolved, it morphed into spyware—a program that you don't know is on your computer that logs everything you do. Key logging spyware captures all your keystrokes, which mean usernames, passwords, sensitive messages, credit card numbers, expiration dates, and the three digit code on the back too.

This is why, from this day forward, you should never use the computer in a hotel business center, the computer in your local copy center, or the computer at your friend's house. You just never know if someone's computer is infected with spyware. Therefore, only use your own computer or your own laptop when you're traveling. The risk is simply too great to use any other computer.

Sometimes IT professionals think their company's computers are free of spyware on them even though they have never examined them. But let me describe one of my favorite things to do when I'm at a business doing a security review.

Recently I went in to do a security review with a company on the West Coast that's a real estate agency. Unfortunately, they let their real estate agents do whatever they want on their computers. That's right...the agents can download programs at will, use instant messenger, and bring in CDs from the outside. The sky's the limit.

While I was there, the IT guy gave me a spiel that I don't hear that often anymore: "You don't need to be here. Everything's secure." During our conversation he mentioned that the machines had instant messenger installed on them. I knew I could win him over, so I said, "Okay, maybe you're right. Maybe I don't need to be here and everything is perfectly secure. But before I leave, can we just go take a look at one machine?"

He says, "Sure, which one?"

"Well, how about somebody who uses instant messenger?"

Since they all used instant messenger, it wasn't very hard to find a computer to use.

So we go over the Marilyn's machine and he says to me, "What do you want to do?"

I reply, "Nothing. I don't touch your keyboards. You're going to do it. I'm going to show you how so you can benefit the most from today's visit."

I believe in the "teach 'em to fish mode." Besides that, I don't want to know any passwords.

So he sits down and logs in, and he says, "Where do you want to go?"

"I'd like you to go to www.webroot.com," I reply.

He types in www.webroot.com, and the computer displays an "error 404: page not found" message.

Now he looks at me and says, "Maybe you meant a different web site address?"

Trust me, www.webroot.com is a good website. So why is the computer saying "error 404: page not found"?

Because of spyware. The computer is infected and it's practicing self-preservation at this point.

So I asked, "You must have at least one computer here that hasn't been used with instant messenger, right?"

He thinks for a moment and says, "There is one machine. We just set it up late last night. I bet nobody has touched it yet."

So we go to that machine. He logs in and types www.webroot. com, and sure enough, up comes Webroot's website.

"Hmmm," is all he says.

So I say, "Okay, here's what I want you to do." I then showed him the file to download, which is basically a free scanning tool that lets you scan to see if you have any spyware on your system. He copies it off onto a CD. We carry it over to Marilyn's machine. We insert the CD and load the software.

And as soon as the scan starts, it identifies Trojans infecting her machine that were active.

Now this IT guy is recognizing the names of the Trojans. He's a good IT guy and knows his stuff. So he dives under the desk and unhooks the Ethernet cable.

Just for grins I ask him, "Why did you do that?"

He says, "I don't want these infecting any of the other machines."

"Do you really think the other machines are immune?" I ask.

At that point he turned pale. Now I had somebody who was glad I was there. I showed him what to do, and we got everything all straightened out.

Another big concern with spyware besides keystroke logging and Trojan software is that you're getting files stored on your system that you don't even know are there. And the way a lot of companies discover this is that they notice their server is filled up and they don't understand why.

If you have to purchase new hard drives because yours are getting filled up and you can't figure out why, that's one of your first clues that you may be infected with spyware.

At this point people always ask, "Is there an easy way to find out if you have extra data stored on your computer?"

It isn't necessarily easy, but if you check all your files to be sure they are what you expect them to be, and you add up the storage space of your files, and then add the free space, then hopefully the number you come up with will match the capacity of your drive (or array). If the number you come up with when you add the total files to the total free space is significantly less than the drive capacity, or if you see files that appear peculiar, you may wish to consult an IT specialist to determine what may be going on.

It is possible for someone to encrypt the data so you can't see it. The files on your machine may be displayed with an extension that looks legit, and it's encrypted with a tool like TrueCrypt. TrueCrypt is a great encryption tool, but it could, of course, be used by bad people as well as good people. So sometimes you have to really go in and search for hidden data.

With that said, though, some hackers are clumsy and will actually store the files as regular movie files, images, or some other obvious file type, and you can spot them more easily.

And again, this is why you have your IT professional working with you. Have them perform a scan and help you figure out what's going on in your machine.

Action Item: Go to www.webroot.com and scan your system for spyware. If your computer won't let you access the site, have your IT professional help you. You may also purchase the program from your local office supply store and install it on your machine immediately.

CHAPTER 22

Tools to Keep Spyware Away from Your Machines

Now that you know about spyware and why you need to keep it off your machines, I'm going to tell you the two recommended tools to keep this spyware problem from happening to you.

Two good tools are SpySweeper from www.webroot.com and Spyware Doctor from www.pctools.com

Both these tools are available in versions that are centrally managed, which your IT professionals will love, because they don't have to personally visit each and every computer every day to perform a scan. The software will do this for them, automatically, and report back to one central station.

Realize, though, that these centrally-managed anti-spyware tools are similar and totally independent of the WSUS tool that manages Microsoft updates for you. Your IT professional will look at the centrally managed anti-spyware report during the ten minute checkup, when they check the WSUS report too, among other reports to be discussed soon.

For example, you would know if all the computers had been scanned for spyware during the night. If Mary Lou's computer didn't scan, you need to go find out why. Did she leave it off? Is she a salesperson who has a laptop, and she forgot to plug it in and turn it on or connect to your network through the night like she's supposed to, so you know your network is safe day-to-day?

Here's how it works: You already have your IT professional or your go-to person doing a ten-minute check every morning. During this time, he or she is looking at WSUS. Also during this time, he or she is going to look at your anti-spyware console to make sure everything is okay there too.

Again, if you are curious, www.webroot.com offers a free scanning tool at their web site. It doesn't delete anything. It just checks for spyware.

The version of www.webroot.com SpySweeper that you pay for will quarantine the questionable files. And then you can decide whether to delete them or keep them. The program is configurable to how you want it to work.

These programs cost around $19 a seat.

You don't need to use both tools. If you do use more than one anti-spyware tool, your computer is likely going to be really slow, probably to the point of frustration for the user.

One of the challenges we're facing right now is that many tools claim to be both anti-virus and anti-spyware. But the problem is, those suites or bundled products don't work as well as the ones that are just anti-spyware or just anti-virus. So use an anti-spyware tool in conjunction with whatever anti-virus tool you like. Hopefully, in the future, the suites that contain both anti-virus and anti-spyware will actually be excellent at performing both tasks.

With all this said, please beware of fake anti-spyware tools on the marketplace. There are sites that pretend to be selling anti-spyware, but the programs they sell are really spyware. So you pay for and download the tool to your machine and think you're protected, but you've really just willingly infected your machine. One very useful list of fake products is the "The Spyware Warrior List of Rogue/Suspect Anti-Spyware Products & Web Sites" at www.spywarewarrior.com.

Along this strategy, when you go to www.webroot.com for the free scan, be sure you actually type the web address in your address bar. Do not use a search engine to find the company's site, since you might end up at a "fake" site pretending to be selling you SpySweeper.

Here's what can happen: One Saturday afternoon I received a call from a client. It was a CEO who attended one of my recent presentations. He quickly explained that he decided to install Webroot at home. He downloaded it over the Internet.

But he didn't listen to me during the presentation. Rather than go directly to www.webroot.com, he Googled Webroot and got over 70 pages in his results. He was confused, so he figured the top one must surely be the right web site. So he clicked on it and downloaded the product.

As it turned out, the file he downloaded was nothing but Trojans, and now his system was shut down. He said he was paying an IT professional to come out to his home on Saturday and rebuild his machine.

I asked, "Why did you call me to tell me this?"

He replied, "Because I want you to promise me that you will keep telling everyone never to put Webroot in their search bar, but to go to www.webroot.com in the address bar. Tell them to listen to you—you are serious!"

Please learn from his mistake. In case you're not sure about the difference between the search bar and address bar, the search bar is powered by a search engine, like Google or Ask. Usually, right next to the search bar, you'll see something that says, "Search." An address bar is sometimes the uppermost bar of your web browser that displays the web page you're viewing. If you're on your home page, the address bar displays the address of your home page. Simply put your cursor in that top address bar, delete the current address it's displaying, and type in www.webroot.com. In Internet Explorer, a shortcut is to type webroot and then hold down the control key and press Enter. This shortcut will automatically add the *http://www* in front and the *.com* at the end.

One additional caution here, though: If you're infected with certain kinds of viruses, they may redirect you to a bogus anti-spyware site, even if you're going to the site directly. This is why, if you suspect your computer is infected, you may want to go to your local software store and buy the program in the box rather than try to download it. Even better, talk to your IT professional. If your machine is infected, there is a good chance that some of the other computers at your office are as well.

When the program is being installed and asks, "May I scan your machine for spyware before installing anti-spyware?"

you answer yes. Likewise, when it asks, "Do you want to check for updates before you install?" you say yes. Because those updates and that scanning are what combat programs that are already on your machine and that try to disable the anti-spyware software as it gets installed. So let your anti-spyware product go through its motions. And when you bring a new machine into your office, put an anti-spyware program on it immediately, before the user ever touches it.

Action Item: In Windows explorer, right click on each drive and choose the "search" option and specify you want to search for pictures and video. See if you notice any suspicious files on your system.

CHAPTER 23

E-mail Security

When I say the word "e-mail," people tend to groan and smile at the same time. Yes, e-mail can be a time-saver and productivity booster, but if it's not used properly, it can also waste time and cause problems in your business. Love it or hate it, though, e-mail is definitely here to stay.

When it comes to e-mail, the first thing you need to understand is that e-mail is more like a postcard rather than a letter in an envelope. That is, unless you're using some form of encryption, your e-mail is *not* secure, and anyone can read it. If you feel having encrypted e-mail would be useful, consider a service such as www.postx.com.

A lot of business people, including CEOs, use their work address e-mail for personal messages, which means there's a record of their personal e-mails on the company's system. In other words, someone in the IT department or elsewhere could, theoretically, go in and read those personal e-mails, distribute them, etc.

Other people opt to use a personal e-mail account, such as an AOL, Google mail, or Yahoo address, but they access those messages on company time, using the company's computers.

In this scenario, unless the company uses special monitoring software, the IT department would not have a record of those personal e-mails to look at. However, one CEO for whom I did a security review found there was a program running on his machine called "When, What, Where," which is a tool that allowed someone to watch every single thing he did— every keystroke, every e-mail, everything displayed on his screen. After some more investigation, we learned that his assistant had this spyware program on her machine too.

When we examined the systems using the installed anti-spyware tool and ran a scan to specifically look for spyware, this program didn't show on the report. Apparently, someone had gone in and white-listed "When, What, Where," meaning as far as the spyware scanning program was concerned, "When, What, Where" was an okay program.

As we probed deeper, we learned that people (we didn't know who yet) were accessing the records to read what was there, and some of them were logging in as an administrator on the domain, suggesting it was someone in the IT department.

At this point in the investigation, the CEO decided, "That's it." He went down to his IT department and confronted them. "Which one of you is doing this?" he asked. All members of the three-person IT team denied any knowledge of the program whatsoever. The CEO's response was to terminate all three.

Now, his actions were against my recommendations. I would never let go of the entire IT team like that. I even go so far as to tell IT departments, "Don't all go to lunch in the same car."

Because if you lose all your IT professionals on the same day, that could devastate your company. When I explained that to the CEO, he replied, "You don't understand. I have to trust my IT professionals. If there's any doubt in my mind, I'm not okay with that." That's why he chose to clean house.

Realize that if someone wants to read e-mail messages, they can intercept the e-mail in many locations along the delivery path. That means at the sending computer, at the e-mail server used to send the mail, along the sender's local area network, at the Internet Service Provider (ISP), and at the same four places on the recipient's side, if not other places as well.

Another problem with e-mail is that people can easily forward messages to other parties. You may have intended your private communication to go to just the recipient, but now the recipient can easily, and often unintentionally, share your private communication with the wrong people.

The point here is that you should never put anything secure through an e-mail. So if you're going to talk with someone about selling your business, for example, do it via phone or in person, but not in an e-mail. Only put things in an e-mail that you wouldn't mind being public knowledge. That's really how insecure e-mail is.

Finally, archiving of e-mail is useful if you ever need to research e-mail correspondence for regulatory compliance, legal discovery, and other reasons. Unless you already have an e-mail archiving solution, consider getting one to protect you. Also, some organization's legal departments actually discourage keeping old e-mail messages.

Action Item: From this day forward, when you put anything in an e-mail, ask yourself if you would feel comfortable with seeing your message on the front page of a newspaper. If not, then call the person, send them a letter, or use some form of encrypted communication.

CHAPTER 24

Anti-Spam Tools

Many people share with me their woes about spam filters and anti-spam software. That's why this chapter will solve your anti-spam issues. Here are the two biggest issues people have with spam filters:

1. Bad e-mail messages get through the filter.
2. Good e-mail messages get caught in the spam filter.

When the bad messages get through, you not only waste time deleting the garbage messages, but you are also vulnerable to viruses. And when good stuff gets caught in your filter and doesn't reach you, you have to look through your spam to find those good messages. In that case, what's the point of even having the spam filter if you have review all the junk anyway?

Here's the answer: Postini.

Postini is a service you subscribe to. For large companies, the yearly fee is around $20 per e-mail account, and for small organizations with ten computers or less, the fee is around $33 per e-mail account.

Postini (www.postini.com) has competitors that you may want to investigate, such as www.mxlogic.com and www.appriver.com. Postini is my favorite though.

Basically, Postini filters your e-mail before it ever arrives at your organization. It's totally outsourced, which is definitely a plus since your IT team is free to work on other tasks. You could also use an appliance on your network, such as the Barracuda spam filter, which is a device (a box) you plug into your network. This appliance is very nice and works very well. Keep in mind that the Barracuda is one more thing for your IT professional to have to take care of. So I would rather you outsource and free up your IT professional.

Another advantage of outsourcing your spam filtering is that in the event your e-mail server crashes, your outsourced anti-spam company can hold your inbound e-mail messages until your e-mail server comes back online.

Some IT professionals are happy with their existing anti-spam solution, yet it takes up five hours of their time per week to manage the filter. This wasted time can include needing to create new filter rules, helping users recover legitimate e-mail messages that were mistakenly deleted by the spam filter (called "false-positives), and dealing with other issues such as reading frequent messages from the anti-spam program telling them "here is the e-mail I deleted in the past hour." If your IT professional has to babysit the anti-spam solution like this, it is all the more reason to switch to something like Postini.

Before we go too far into spam filtering and Postini, I want to make one thing perfectly clear: If your current spam filter is working fine, and it's not letting in bad e-mails or keeping good e-mails from reaching you, and your IT professional never has to worry about it, then you're probably already using a service that outsources to Postini, or you have something else that's working well enough for your needs, so don't mess with it. But if you're not happy with what you're doing now, then it's probably time for a change.

So, how does Postini work? First, they do the basics, such as scan the message for foul language, words on the "bad word" list, and any of the sixty-five different ways you can spell Viagra using numbers and symbols, among other things. Then they do things that are secret, because if the spammers knew everything Postini did, the spammers would find a way around the filtering devices.

However, one of the things I know Postini does is to set up "honey pots" around the world. A honey pot is a server that pretends to be a corporation. It looks like a corporation from the outside, but it's really just a server with a bogus corporation name.

Any e-mail that is sent to that honey pot automatically gets blocked from ever getting to you, because Postini knows it is spam. That "honey pot" corporation never requested an e-mail from anyone. So if they're getting an e-mail, it has to be spam. Therefore, that same message and sender will never make it to your inbox. That's just one of many things Postini has in place to keep you spam-free.

Now, here's how Postini "fits" in with your e-mail server. Remember, this is something completely outsourced, so there's no hardware you have to buy. Typically, when someone sends you an e-mail, the message goes from the sender, to your e-mail server, and then to you. When you have Postini, rather than the message going directly to your e-mail server, it first goes to Postini. They'll scan the message and make sure it's not spam. If it's a good e-mail, it will be delivered immediately to your e-mail server and then on to you. If it's a bad e-mail, you'll never see it unless you choose to go examine the e-mail that Postini captured for you.

Getting the e-mail to go to Postini first is something you will want your IT professional to help you with. In simple terms, your IT professional will change part of your DNS record called the MX record, which stands for mail exchanger. Your MX record tells the Internet, "Hey, if you have mail destined for me@myemailaddress.com, here's where you send it." Now you're simply telling the Internet to send your mail to Postini instead of to you. Then Postini will send the cleaned e-mail to your e-mail server, which will then send it to you the next time you check your e-mail. Yes, it sounds complicated and like a long process, but remember, this is cyberspace. All this message transferring happens in mere seconds.

One thing you will want to do, though, is configure your e-mail server to only accept e-mail from Postini's address. Why? Because some spammers are smart. They'll send mail not only to you@yourcompanyname.com, but they'll also send spam to you@60.173.85.99, or whatever your company's IP address is. In that case, they circumvent DNS, and the spam e-mail message would go straight to your e-mail server, and then straight to you. As long as your e-mail server is configured to only accept e-mail messages from Postini, then the spammer's message will be rejected.

Some companies use an e-mail hosting company. If your company does this, and the company that hosts your e-mail says they can't accept e-mail from Postini only, then you need to either find a hosting company that will or bring an Exchange server in-house that you can configure the way you want. AppRiver does offer hosting along with their spam filtering.

If you run into the situation where your e-mails aren't getting to people—that you're ending up in people's spam mail filter—then make sure you're not on any blacklists. One way to find out is to go to a site www.DNSstuff.com. There you'll find many useful tools, one of which will let you see if you're on any blacklists.

Imagine how much more productive you and your co-workers could be without all that spam passing into your inbox and without searching your spam filter for messages you should have gotten. Give these tools a try so you can reclaim your inbox once and for all.

Action Item: Unless you are just ecstatic with your existing anti-spam solution, try out the 30 day trial from www.postini.com or one of the other hosted anti-spam providers.

CHAPTER 25

Trojan Horses

A Trojan horse is a program that looks useful in an effort to have users download and install it on their computers. However, that program (unknown to you) also has some form of malicious intent as well. While Trojan horses may appear to be useful or interesting programs to an unsuspecting user, they are actually harmful when executed. One example could be a screensaver program downloaded from the Internet. The free screensaver sure seems useful (and cool!), but hiding underneath may be another program designed to do any number of things, including capturing your passwords and credit card numbers, sending out spam around the world, or storing pornographic images on your hard drive without your knowledge.

Many identity theft cases can be traced back to the victim using a computer infected with a key logging Trojan that captured their keystrokes. The victim may have been on vacation using a computer in an Internet Café, or their own computer may have been infected. The user enters their username and password to their bank, for example, and they don't realize that someone else is also reading that information as they type it. Unfortunately, many people often have a false sense of security when using a computer.

They think it's completely secure because nothing "strange" happens on screen, all the while they're unknowingly giving out their person information to thieves.

Another common type of Trojan horse is a spam Trojan, where the malicious program takes over your computer to send out spam. The biggest problem with this is that you (or your company) get blacklisted. This means that, as far as the organizations watching for spammers are concerned, your company is a spammer since spam is originating from your address. So now anytime you or anyone else in your organization tries to send a legitimate e-mail, many people can't get your legitimate messages because you've been blacklisted. Your organization has been labeled as a spammer.

Another type of Trojan is a porn Trojan. That's when hackers store files on your system that you didn't know were there. The most commonly stored files are pornography. In this instance, people who don't want to get caught with questionable images on their computer hard drive use an unsuspecting computer as their personal storage unit. That means even if you have never in your life visited a pornographic web site or had pornography displayed on your monitor, someone can be storing those images on your computer without you ever knowing it.

I wish I could say that porn Trojans are rare, but I can't. Many organizations have them on their system. They may notice that their hard drives in their servers keep filling up, or that their Internet connections seem to slow down dramatically due to a tremendous amount of traffic. Eventually they figure out that their servers are being used as porn Trojans.

So what can you do? Well, there are actually utilities available that enable you to look for pictures on your computer and in your e-mail that have flesh tones. However, the hackers have gotten wise to this and a lot of Internet porn today now has people who look green or red.

One of the best solutions to avoid Trojan programs is to apply all of the protective methods in this book. Security works best in layers, one layer on top of the next. All of these pieces fit together to solve the puzzle that can help keep your network secure.

Another option that will help protect from Trojans is to block most, if not all, e-mail attachments. Consider whether your employees really need to be sending and receiving attachments that are graphical in nature. Do they need to send and receive pictures at all? If not, then you could block pictures from e-mail. If someone wants to send or receive pictures of their family, they should be using their personal account anyway, since family pictures are not work-related.

Another type of attachment to rule out is an executable attachment. Executable means that the attachment is a program of some kind. Normally, there is no reason to send an executable attachment unless the sender is, knowingly or unknowingly, wanting to spread a Trojan or other type of malicious code. Many firewalls provide an option to delete attachments and your IT professional will know, or can easily find out, which ones to delete.

So while you may not be able to totally eliminate Trojans from getting on your network, you can significantly diminish the risk.

But the bottom line is, if you end up with a key-logging Trojan, spam Trojan, a porn Trojan, or some other malicious program, you will suffer damages. That damage can't be un-done. In every case, the best solution is to prevent an infection like this from happening to begin with. Trojan infections almost always result in negative outcomes, so take the steps to keep your system clean.

Action Item: Visit with your IT professional about blocking all e-mail attachments at your organization, or possibly allowing only .pdf attachments, or maybe only blocking executable attachments. Discuss which strategy will be most appropriate for your organization and then see that it is implemented.

CHAPTER 26

Rootkits

Rootkits are the next level up from viruses and spyware. A rootkit works like Darth Vader in Star Wars using the dark side of the force. Rootkit viruses hide on your computer like an invisible menace designed to wreak havoc on your system. Here's a simplified explanation of how a rootkit works: Whenever your anti-virus program is scanning through files in search of danger and it comes to a rootkit program file, the rootkit is able to tell the anti-virus package, "No, you did not mean to scan this file. You meant that file over there." The rootkit points the anti-virus scan on to the next file in line. And your anti-virus program says, "Oh, okay. I did not mean this file. I meant that file over there." So your anti-virus program will never scan the rootkit virus file, meaning your anti-virus program will never report that you have a virus.

The rootkit does the same thing to your anti-spyware scanning program. Some rootkits also hide themselves from being displayed in your Task Manager, a tool designed to show you the processes running on your computer at any given moment. You have likely seen your Task Manager when you did a Ctrl+Alt+Delete to reboot your computer. Before restarting, the Task Manager popped up and displayed which programs were running and which were not responding. You can actually examine your Task Manager at any time, not just when you do a hard reboot. When you examine Task Manager, you will see lots of programs running, but none of them are the rootkit since the rootkit has tricked Task Manager into not knowing it is there. This "stealth" behavior is one of the things that make rootkits particularly dangerous.

While we are on the topic of Task Manger, be sure to check out Process Explorer from www.sysinternals.com as a replacement to Task Manager. Normally tools like this are only of interest to IT professionals, although you may be interested in seeing one of the nicest tools available and telling your IT professional about it in case no one ever has told them before. The rootkits may be able to fool Process Explorer as well, but Process Explorer works very well to show you information about the processes running on your machine.

The above mentioned www.Sysinternals.com is one of the best websites ever created for IT professionals who are supporting Microsoft products. Microsoft purchased the site a while back, but part of the purchase agreement is that they will leave the site up and running. Hopefully the site will be maintained and the tools will be updated as operating systems evolve.

On www.sysinternals.com you can find a useful tool called rootkit revealer. So if your computer is behaving in such a way that you strongly suspect it is infected with something—you can just tell by the way it's acting—but your anti-virus says your computer is clean and the anti-spyware says it's clean, then you can use rootkit revealer to see if the computer is infected with a rootkit. Once you find out which one is on your machine, you can know what you're dealing with and take appropriate steps to get rid of it.

It is worth noting that there is such a thing as a "good" rootkit. So you'll want to talk over your rootkit revealer findings with your IT professional. Some legitimate programs, especially anti-virus programs, will use rootkits as part of their protection scheme. Hiding your anti-virus program from hacking tools makes it more difficult for a virus to deactivate your anti-virus package.

Sony Music got in trouble for using rootkits. Some Sony audio CDs were configured in such a way that when a listener played the audio CD in a computer, the audio CD would store a rootkit program on the user's computer to limit the number of copies the user could make of the CD. This program was installed on the computer without the user's permission or knowledge. So, in a way, you could say that Sony was infecting computers with rootkits. Then a programmer found a way that the Sony rootkit could be exploited by a hacker to gain unauthorized access to the user's computer. As a result, Sony responsibly offered a patch to computer users. This is well documented on the Internet if you want to learn more.

Notice that the "solution tool" is called rootkit *revealer* and not rootkit *remover*. When a computer becomes infected with a malicious rootkit, it is often very difficult to remove the rootkit file. Often, the fastest solution is to erase all the information on the machine and totally rebuild the machine from scratch. This is where having current images of machines in your backups can help a lot. Image backup will be discussed soon.

Action Item: If your computer is behaving like it has an infection of some kind, and your anti-virus software and anti-spyware software tell you the computer is clean, then use rootkit revealer to look for a rootkit on the system.

CHAPTER 27

Firewalls

A firewall is an IT security device and/or software that is configured to either permit or deny traffic and connections to and from the Internet or specific programs. In even more simple terms, a firewall lets good data through and blocks unwanted data. You want to be sure you have a firewall protecting your entire network, as well as firewall software on individual workstations.

When we build a home or a business, we generally try to find a "good neighborhood." When we travel, we try to stay away from "bad neighborhoods" for our own safety. Realize that once a computer is connected to the Internet, that computer is directly connected to good and bad neighborhoods alike. Computers and networks must be protected at all times.

First, let's address the firewall that separates your network from the Internet. If your company is small, your router and your firewall may be in the same appliance. If your company is large, you will likely have a dedicated firewall, maybe even more than one. I've seen some companies have up to five firewalls, each from a different manufacturer. The logic is that if a virus is so new that most firewalls don't recognize the malicious traffic as "bad," hopefully at least one of the other firewalls will be recently updated and still protect the network. As mentioned earlier, the use of new malicious code before firewalls and anti-virus products realize the code is malicious is called a "Zero Day Attack."

Firewalls are constantly improving in their capabilities, because hackers are constantly thinking of new ways to attack. Talk to your IT professional to be sure your firewall is up-to-date and protects you using deep packet inspection. Also make sure your firewall can protect you from fragmentation attacks. Earlier firewalls would watch for malicious code coming in a message that says something like "delete all data on the server." For a simple explanation of how a fragmentation attack works, consider a situation in which the malicious code is sent in two parts. The first message says "delete all" and the second message says "data on the server." Unless the firewall is configured to watch for this kind of fragmentation attack, it will look at the two messages independently and will allow each part through since, by itself, each part of the message seems harmless enough. When it puts the message together, the server would perform an unwanted action. That's what you want your firewall to prevent.

One of my clients actually uses not one, not two, but five firewalls in a row to protect his organization. Each firewall is produced and updated by a different manufacturer. This way they have a first opinion, a second opinion, all the way to a fifth opinion on whether the incoming data is safe. While this may seem like, and quite possibly is, overkill, this company is very happy with their choice. Their billable time is $10,000 per hour, so if any malicious code makes it into their organization and stops their users from working, they can easily lose $80,000 per day. This risk is so great that they feel the "insurance" of having five firewalls is well worth the investment. All of the firewalls they use are very fast and there is no noticeable latency for Internet traffic because of the multiple firewalls.

Other organizations use multiple firewalls to provide different zones of protection. For example, there may be two firewalls between the internal trusted network and the Internet. The company's web server may sit between the two firewalls in what is referred to as a DMZ. The firewall closest to the Internet is designed to allow the public through to access the web server and only block malicious content. Then, the firewall that separates the DMZ from the trusted network is much more restrictive about what information is allowed into the corporate network.

Your network's perimeter firewall filters all electronic traffic, both incoming and outgoing, to and from your company. For example, if someone in your company wants to use instant messenger, and you have decided that IM is not allowed, you would configure your firewall to prevent that employee's computer from sending or receiving instant messenger messages through the Internet. You can essentially program the firewall to allow or disallow data to flow both into and out of your company and, depending on the level of sophistication of your firewall, even control this on a user-by-user or computer-by-computer basis.

When used properly, a firewall can indeed keep lots of bad things from getting into your network. The scary thing is that there are ways a malicious program can completely circumvent your firewall. One way works like this: Someone brings in a computer from the outside, such as a laptop a salesperson uses while on the road, and plugs into your system. If that computer got infected with anything while the salesperson had it out on the road, as soon as it's connected to the network, the entire network can be infected and the perimeter firewall could do nothing about it. That's why you also need a software firewall on every workstation.

Often, this individual software firewall is an add-on to the anti-virus software you're already using. So if you're using Trend Micro or Symantec, for example, you pay an extra fee to have a firewall also installed at each workstation (sometimes it's already included in your license and you don't have to pay anything).

The moment I recommend putting a firewall program on each workstation, a lot of IT professionals start to panic. They're concerned that once that software firewall is on the workstations, all the users are going to get pop-up messages from the firewall for every program that attempts to access the Internet or do something else the firewall doesn't like. The pop-up generally asks something like, "Is it okay if this program accesses the Internet?"

And for most end users, when they see any pop-up on their screen, the first thing they're going to do is call IT. Then the IT professionals will get a flood of calls: "My computer has this message up. What should I do?" So that means if you have 50 users in your organization, and each user gets ten of these pop-ups a day, that's 500 new phone calls a day to IT.

No wonder the IT professionals start panicking at the idea of workstation firewalls.

Here's the solution: Rather than put the firewall on every computer all at once, just install the firewall on one user's workstation initially. Then have a user sit at the machine and use it the way he or she normally does so IT can find out what pop-ups are going to occur. Then IT can centrally white list or centrally black list those programs for the firewall. For example, maybe you need to tell the firewall that it's okay for Outlook to go to the Internet but it's not okay for instant messenger to access the Internet.

And so you build your central white list and your central black list to the point that users don't get pop-ups anymore. After that user's computer no longer displays pop-ups, roll the firewall out on to a couple more computers. See if those users get any pop-ups. If they do, centrally white list or blacklist as appropriate. Then you ultimately will get to roll the firewall out to all your workstations.

Having these personal workstation firewalls is so important. For example, if a hacker wants to perform a targeted attack on your company, one thing they could do is leave a few USB memory sticks on the ground outside your building or in the parking lot. They're banking on the fact that at least one of those sticks will make it inside the building and into a computer. And once that happens, if there's no individual firewall in place, the hacker has a much easier way into the company's network.

This actually happened to a medical facility. Someone put eight USB sticks in their parking lot. As employees arrived, some would find memory sticks on the ground, feel curious about the contents, carry them into the building, and plug them into a workstation. Six of them made it into the facility and into computers, and each of them had a Trojan on it. So as soon as the USB memory stick got plugged in, the team who put the memory sticks in the parking lot was able to get in remotely and control that machine. That's why you need a firewall on every machine—to help reduce the likelihood of such an attack being successful.

Action Item: Check with your IT professional to find out if software firewalls are installed on every workstation and if they are centrally updated and monitored on a daily basis. If not, have the personal firewalls deployed right away in stages as described in this chapter.

CHAPTER 28

Virtual Private Networks

Virtual Private Networks (or VPN for short) enable remote computers to connect through the Internet as if they had a long Ethernet network cable stretched all the way from the remote computers back to your company's main office. This connection is helpful in connecting remote satellite offices as well as employees out in the field to the company's network.

One advantage of having remote offices and employees connecting through a VPN is so that your IT professionals can update and support the remote machines automatically using the centrally managed tools you already utilize at your main location. If you don't have a VPN for your company, one of your employees could be traveling on Patch Tuesday and not get a needed update until the next time he or she is physically in your main office. This could be a long time, depending on how extensively that person travels. That would make that computer vulnerable for an unnecessary period of time.

With a VPN established, you could mandate that everyone who is out in the field with a laptop must connect to the company's network every night, or at the very least, every three days. Some companies even give their employees wireless cards from companies such as Sprint or Verizon so they can be connected from virtually anywhere there is service. Then as long as the laptop is connected, and the VPN established, IT can run their security updates, anti-virus, anti-spyware, and personal firewall checks on the computer even though it's not physically in the office. (As a side note, if someone is out in the field with a laptop and wants to keep the laptop synchronized with his or her desktop office computer, they can do so with tools such as Microsoft Briefcase, Microsoft SyncToy, as well as www.secondcopy.com.)

This simple VPN will help prevent one of your employees from coming back to the office and bringing viruses and other malicious items into the company's network, because IT has a chance to regularly update, monitor, and service the machine. And best of all, the cost is very inexpensive and often based on the number of users connecting through the VPN.

Using a VPN has an additional security benefit in that it is one way of providing encryption to the data being transmitted. Why is this important? Because there is a tool available called Cain & Abel, which allows someone to connect into a network, such as one at a hotel, and run an "ARP poisoning" attack. This program basically tells all the computers on the connection, "Hey, the place you've been going to—the place you think is the Internet—really isn't the real Internet. I'm the real Internet."

Then, all the computers on that network, be it in a hotel, coffee shop, or wherever, won't question this new information. They simply start sending all the data that they would normally send to the Internet to transmit to the new place, which is a hacker's computer. This is called a "person in the middle attack." After all the data gets relayed to this person's computer, the attacker's computer, which is running Cain and Abel, then forwards the data to the real Internet. The only thing people on the network notice is that their Internet speed slowed down a little.

For the hacker, it's like being on a reality TV show. He or she sees everything going on with the people connected to the wireless network. "Oh, look at that e-mail. That person's cat died. That's too bad. Oh, this other guy is selling his business. Wonder if I could sell that information to someone? Oh, look where that guy's surfing. I wonder is his company knows he's looking at porn while on the clock."

The hacker watches everything...credit card numbers, passwords, logins...everything. That's why you will benefit from using some form of encryption on your data when you connect to any of those networks in a hotel, coffee shop, or anywhere else. A VPN is one way to provide this encryption. This is just another reason to seriously consider a VPN for all remote connections to your company.

For remote users, the process of connecting to the VPN normally consists of two steps. First, connect to the Internet. Next, establish the VPN connection to the office through the Internet. Your IT professionals may be able to make this a single step process, and users at remote offices often have a VPN connection that is operating 100% of the time so there are no additional connection steps necessary.

Action Item: If you have remote satellite offices and/or people who connect from off-site locations to your network, have discussions with your IT professionals about securing those connections through a VPN. This would allow remote management and help protect your users from a "person in the middle attack."

CHAPTER 29

Content Blocking and Internet Monitoring

If your company has Internet access, then odds are you also have employees who abuse their Internet privileges. Whether they're online planning their vacation, searching employment sites, checking their horoscope or the latest sports scores, or even going to gambling or pornography sites, they're lowering their productivity and potentially abusing the company's Internet connection.

To make matters worse, some web sites even have a so-called "boss button." The premise is that if you notice your boss approaching your cubicle or work area, you simply click the "boss button" and the web site you were viewing disappears and up pops an article on time management or some other business development topic. Then when your boss walks away, with the click of a mouse you can continue on the real site you were visiting.

Unfortunately, even "casual" misuse costs your company thousands of dollars each year. A recent survey about Internet usage conducted by IntelliQuest Information Group found that the average amount of time a user spends online for personal use has grown from an average of 6.9 hours per week to a current average of 9.8 hours per week. Also, 46% of the online population of 57 million adults accessed the Internet from work at least some of that time. The percentage of time your employees spend on the Internet that is not business-related is the amount your company loses in salary expenses due to lost productivity.

To put it in better perspective, if an employee who earns $35,000 annually is spending 20% of his or her time being unproductive on the Internet, that equals $7,000 lost out of your payroll. Add to that 20% of your organization's share of Social Security payments, unemployment taxes, and worker's compensation insurance, and the true amount lost can be staggering.

Fortunately, you have options to curb the abuse and get people back in the productivity lane: Content Blocking and Internet Tracking.

Just as their names imply, content blocking tools actually block people from accessing specific sites, and Internet tracking tools allow you to track where people have visited online. Internet tracking and blocking tools give you a menu of services you can choose from that can be effective for curbing Internet abuse.

I personally use LivePrism (www.LivePrism.com) both at home and at the office, and there are many options available for you to choose from. Let's look at three of the most useful menu items from these tools.

First, with the content blocking, you can opt to block porn sites, gambling sites, hate sites, job hunting sites, etc.

Note that you may not want block job hunting sites from all of your employees, just most of them! Therefore, you can selectively block different employees based on their access needs.

When I perform consulting for organizations and examine their IT systems, there is normally a flurry of IT security activity right after my visit as the company makes recommended changes to their network. Then the security work falls off and there tends to be another flurry of activity right before I arrive for the next visit. During one of those repeat visits recently, a polite and concerned CEO stuck his head into the office where I was meeting with the IT team. He said: "What happened? I can't get to my wine web sites and I need to order a gift for a friend."

The IT professional who had enabled content blocking sheepishly responded, "Oh, I blocked access to alcohol sites for everyone on the Internet." He immediately logged into the system and opened up alcohol sites for the CEO. A few minutes later the CEO stuck his head in the office again saying, "Thanks! It works now!" After the CEO left, I asked the IT professional, "Does he smoke cigars too?" The IT professional grinned and his fingers started flying over the keyboard to open up tobacco sites for the CEO as well. This shows how easily IT can block sites and content on a case-by-case basis.

Content blocking software used to be unreliable, as it would block people from going to sites they legitimately needed to visit. But today the technology is much better. The key here is to be able to make "exceptions" for specific teams or individuals on a necessary basis, and also needing to invest only a very small amount of time administering the tools.

The second menu option worth considering is called alerting, which functions whether or not you have selected to block specific sites. With alerting, you and anyone you specify will get notifications when someone visits or attempts to visit sites and categories of sites you have specified. This way you can be alerted when an employee may be attempting to perform some inappropriate action using the Internet at work without your having to monitor the logs constantly.

Alerting can be a very useful tool, as one of my clients found out. This particular CEO used Websense to monitor his employees' Internet use. Soon after he installed the tool, he got an alert that one of his key executives had been at a porn site for ninety minutes and that he viewed over one hundred different pages. With that much activity, it was apparent that this executive didn't stumble upon a porn site by accident.

The CEO had to figure out what to do. He knew that however he treated this one key executive, who he greatly valued, that was how he was going to have to treat everybody else in the future who got caught doing this.

This CEO chose to send out a blanket memo to everyone in the company. The memo read: "Last week someone, who for now will go unnamed, was at a pornographic web site noon to 2 p.m. and viewed over one hundred different pornography pages. We have a record of all of it. If this kind of Internet activity occurs again to anyone in the company, you will be terminated immediately. We are not going to have a "three strikes and you're out" policy here. Our policy is that if you go to a porn site, you're done, with no recourse.'"

Later that day three people came to his office and apologized. And yes, that key executive who triggered the whole thing was one of them.

So learn from this CEO. If you're going to monitor and get alerts, then decide what you're going to do ahead of time should someone visit a site that's prohibited on company time. Then, notify people ahead of time that you're monitoring their activity. Check with your legal advisor about your responsibilities in the notification process.

Now for the third menu item: These tools have an additional benefit, called logging, that could actually save your company hundreds of thousands of dollars in lawsuits. Consider this incident: One of my clients had a female employee who had been working at the company for three weeks. One day she sued the company for sexual harassment. Her statement said, "I walked behind Bob's desk and he was looking at porn. I felt very uncomfortable when I saw the porn on Bob's screen. So I'm suing you for sexual harassment."

Most companies would have to settle out of court, and this woman would have been able to retire. Fortunately, this company was using monitoring software and was able to go back and pull Bob's records. They saw that Bob wasn't even on the Internet during the time she said he was looking at porn. They looked back further and found out that since the day Bob was hired, which had been a long time, he had never been to a porn site—not even once. The company had their lawyer write her lawyer a letter, and that was it. She dropped the lawsuit and quit her job. They never saw her again.

Thank goodness that company had the monitoring software in place.

So you can configure your monitoring software to give you a listing of every web site every employee visits. But as with any tool, you need to use some common sense with it. That is, if one of your employees goes to a travel booking site, like Expedia, and then minimizes the window and walks away, your report could show that the person was on Expedia for many hours. But don't get alarmed with the employee just yet. You have to look to see the number of Expedia pages the person visited. If he or she was on the same page for four hours, that's a good indication that the page was simply running in the background. So use common sense when deciphering your reports. Some more advanced tools can actually help you in this determination by indicating, besides the number of pages visited, the amount of time the mouse was moving around on the page, number of clicks, etc.

Other tools can even capture screen shots, keystrokes, etc. using the concepts behind spyware that were mentioned earlier.

When you choose to implement the Internet blocking, alerting, and monitoring tools, you will have many choices. For example, you can choose to have a server with Websense software running on your network, which is installed locally. Or, as another option, you can use a remote service such as www.LivePrism.com. That means all the traffic in your company has to go out through LivePrism before it gets to the Internet.

The end user interface is similar on either one. The only difference is that when you have something like Websense installed on your server, your IT professionals have to take care of it. If you use an outsourced tool such as LivePrism, then that company has to take care of it. They have to deal with the hacker attacks and other things that could happen. I generally lean toward services that free up your IT professionals' time rather than add "one more server or program" for them to take care of.

Another important point to mention is that both of these options can be configured to include your remote users. That way if you have someone out in the field with a laptop, their machine can still be blocked or monitored.

Often one of the biggest hurdles to implementing Internet blocking, alerting, and monitoring is the organization's existing culture. Often the executives wish to provide a "we are all family" type of environment where everyone is given free rein on their own Internet access. This admirable level of trust may work, at least for a while, but unfortunately, if any employee makes a series of poor choices on the Internet one day, irreparable damage may already be done and there won't be any going back at that point. Now, before anything happens, is the only time that steps toward prevention are an option.

Take, for example, the incident mentioned earlier in which Bob was unjustly accused of viewing porn sites at work. If there hadn't been tracking software in place already, then everyone in the company would have wondered whether Bob had indeed been at such a site. But since the company had taken steps ahead of time, Bob's name was cleared from the unjust accusations.

Action Item: While the choice is ultimately yours, I strongly encourage you to try a thirty day free trial with one of the content blocking, alerting, and monitoring services such as www.liveprism.com or www.websense.com.

CHAPTER 30

Hiring Process to Prevent Internet Abuse

In order to prevent Internet abuse, I recommend that companies have a written checklist that all new hires sign off on. Some items to include in this checklist are:

- Appropriate and inappropriate use of the equipment, including web sites visited and e-mail content

- Standard ways to reduce the likelihood of contracting and spreading malicious software such as viruses and spyware

- The policy regarding bringing personal laptops and personal software into the office

- Who to contact if they suspect a security issue of any kind

- Explain that the Internet is a business tool and should only be used as such. Express the costs associated with providing Internet access and state why the policy must be as stringent as it is— i.e.: to reduce legal liabilities and protect the company's image

- Prohibit employees from using the Internet or e-mail to promote their personal cause or agenda

- Prohibit obscene, harassing, dishonest, profane, or offensive communication of any kind

- Define the password creation/change procedures

- State if and when Internet Relay Chat (IRC) Channels and/or instant messaging may be used

- Explain that all data received, created, and/or sent over the network is the property of the company and is public information without privacy of any kind

- Address the issue of employees using personal devices, like their own modems and portable devices (wireless phones and/or wireless Internet browsers) while at work

- Reserve the right to access all data and monitor activity for any reason or even no reason at all

- Explain who is authorized to access e-mail messages, Internet history, and other monitored data

- Explain the disposition of e-mail messages when the employee is on temporary but extended leave

- Reserve the right to turn over any and all data to law enforcement without prior consent of the sender or receiver

- State the retention/purge schedule for files, including retention procedures for possible use as legal evidence

Action Item: Talk with your company's attorney about what you can and can not have someone sign as a new hire. Then, put your checklist together and implement it. Have your existing staff sign it as well as any newcomers from this day on.

CHAPTER 31

Domain Policies

O f all the things in Microsoft Windows server operating systems, domain policies are my favorite server tool. I love domain policies. I get excited just thinking about domain policies. Okay, you may think I'm a computer geek now, but after you learn what domain policies are, you'll love them too.

Domain policies eliminate problems that are likely costing your company thousands of dollars a year. If you're a big company, the cost may be tens of thousands of dollars a year. IT professionals call the problems each a PEBKAC. Now, I don't care what size company you have, I know that PEBKACs are eating up your money. PEBKACs are causing you to have a larger IT staff than you need, or are causing your right-sized staff to be overworked and behind on their schedules.

So, what's a PEBKAC? Great question. PEBKAC stands for "Problem Exists Between Keyboard And Chair." In other words, user problems.

Here are some of the favorite PEBKACs. The user will delete their printer. Then they call IT and say, "I can't print." IT shows up and asks, "What did you do?" The user replies, "Nothing." Domain policies can prevent this type of PEBKACK by preventing people from ever deleting their printer to begin with.

Unfortunately, all users seem to be programmed that "if a print job doesn't print, then just send hit the print button again…and again…and again…and again." This "send the print job ten times to see if that helps" is a form of PEBKAC that domain policies can't protect against. Often stacks of paper are wasted once the whole line of print jobs make it to the printer for printing.

Another common PEBKAC is when the user changes the background color on their computer screen to blue, and then changes the color of the text font to blue as well. As you can imagine, this results in a perfectly blank looking blue screen. The words are there, but nobody can see them. Again, an urgent call is placed to tech support. An IT professional responds, asks the end user what they did, and gets the standard response, "Nothing." Domain policies can prevent this PEBKAC, allowing both the user and the IT professional to be more productive with their time.

One of my clients had a productivity problem in their shop because the employees had installed "deer hunter" software on the shop floor computer. No one besides your IT professional should have permission to install applications on computers, and domain policies can enforce this for you.

Other PEBKACs include deleting drive mappings, changing screen settings, installing unauthorized software, or performing some other action that results in their computers becoming unstable in one way or another.

Domain policies will prevent that and much more from happening, including eliminating the danger of employees having photographs of scantily clad movie stars set as their desktop image on their computer screen.

Best of all, domain policies are absolutely free. They're built in. You already bought them when you bought the Windows operating system. So please use policies.

You can customize each setting by Domain, Organization Unit, and Site. These three Active Directory objects make sense to your IT professionals. This allows different settings to be applied for different departments, locations, and even individual users. Here are some things I recommend companies use domain policies for:

- Restrict items that appear on the desktop and start menu.
- Require strong passwords, changed regularly, with a minimum length.
- Restrict most if not all the control panel applets and other settings.
- Restrict allowed applications, in particular omitting authorization to run "setup," "install," or any other program that would allow the user to add new software.
- Disable registry editing tools.
- Force the terminal to lock after five minutes of inactivity and require a password to log in again.

- Redirect user's folders to network drives instead of their local C: drive.
- Create a login banner. (I'll explain this in detail shortly.)
- Restrict any other items you deem appropriate.

In short, you can restrict what programs people are allowed to use. You can disable the "install" and "setup" programs so you don't have the problem of users bringing in programs from home and installing them in your office. Not only are these outside programs time wasters for people, but they're likely not licensed for more than one machine. We'll talk more about licensing in an upcoming chapter.

Don't let the users install anything. Make it so that they have to go to IT to get programs installed. Don't let them put on screen savers or anything not business related.

In a sense, domain policies force people to have to use their work computer for work. (And isn't that what you pay them for anyway?) In fact, my recommendation is that when a user sits down at any of your computers, he or she sees four options: Start, Word, Outlook, and Shut Down. They can't do anything else. If anyone needs any other programs, then the IT department can easily enable those programs on an "as needed" basis for individuals or groups of people.

Often IT people give me some version of the following history: "I tried to use policies once, but as soon as one of the executives found out he couldn't get to solitaire anymore, he came into my office and told that that unless I removed all restrictions on network computers I would lose my job." It is very important for the IT department to obtain and receive executive support before deploying domain policies. In this instance, a much better choice than disabling all policies would have been to enable solitaire for the single executive who "needs it" and restrict all the other users.

Earlier I mentioned a "Login Banner." This is a set a log-in message informing the user (using wording based on the advice of your legal advisor) that:

- The computer is to be used for work only.
- The users will be monitored and the user has no privacy on the system.
- All work users create belongs to the company.
- All unauthorized use and access is prohibited.
- Unauthorized users may face civil and criminal penalties.
- If deemed necessary, anything can and will be turned over to law enforcement without asking permission or giving notification.

   (It is important to note that the Foster Institute cannot provide legal advice, so please check with your legal advisors for direction in this area.)

Some CEOs choose to not use such a message, as it feels threatening to some users. Just verify with your legal department what you need to do, and make a conscious choice. By skipping the banner, you may destroy your ability to appropriately handle incidents.

About ten years ago, I had a client that outsourced all their IT work to my company, a common service for us to offer back then. Their computers needed daily support. My costs for supporting the client were becoming astronomical. This was in the days of Novell Netware, and polices were still in their infancy. We deployed them using Netware, restricted every user from only being able to access their word processor, e-mail client, and corporate financial and records database. Miraculously, all of a sudden, the client's network began behaving beautifully! Before, PEBCAKs were causing a technician to need to visit their company every day, and now—after a simple deployment of basic policies—the client was ecstatic. Policies are a beautiful thing!

When deploying polices, be sure to roll them out gradually. First deploy them to a test computer, then to a single user, then a single department or group, and then work up to the entire organization. This way if the policy has some unexpected result, everyone in your organization won't be negatively affected. It is always better to find problems with a small test group so any obstacles can be ironed out early.

Action Item: Ask your IT professionals, "What percentage of your time, on a daily basis, do you spend solving PEBCAK issues?" Don't be surprised if you hear answers of 30% or more. Now, calculate how much money PEBCAKs are costing you in IT expense as well as lost productivity for the employees. Then deploy policies in a staged rollout to reduce this costly expense.

CHAPTER 32

Administrative Accounts and NTFS Permissions

It's extremly important for administrators to only log in to the domain as an administrator when there is a need to perform administrative activities. The rest of the time, the administrator should log in to the domain using a normal account. That way, if a virus or other malware is active when the administrator logs in to the domain at "user level" access, the malware will only have access to areas that the users normally have access to.

Therefore, each person who needs administrative access should have two login usernames and two passwords—one for each user account. For example, the user Barry will have another login account called BarryA. Barry will log in as Barry 90% of the time, and when he needs administrative access, he can log in as BarryA and then log out when he is finished administrating the network.

Also, if more than one user needs administrative access, give each user his or her own administrative logon rather than sharing one common administrator account. This way, with auditing, you will be able to track which administrative users do what. And if someone ever leaves the company, that person's account can be disabled without affecting the other administrative accounts.

NTFS Permissions

Equally important is to have all data on all drives, partitions, and folders restricted to allow access only on a "Need to Know" basis. Therefore, ensure that your users, groups, and NTFS permissions are configured appropriately.

While a case can be made for share level permissions in some circumstances, NTFS permissions are more flexible and can provide more security. Remember that share level permissions can be completely bypassed if the user logs on locally to the computer in person or through remote desktop, while NTFS permissions function no matter where the user is logged on. NTFS also allows special handling of inheritance between parent and sub-folders.

Within the share level permissions and within the NTFS permissions themselves, the least restrictive access is always granted unless "deny" has been activated for the user and/or a group that contains the user.

Then, once Microsoft determines the resultant share permissions and the resultant NTFS permissions, Microsoft will use the "most restrictive" of the two. That means that NTFS may show "full control"; however the share level permissions may be set to "read only," resulting in "read only" permissions for that group or user (as long as the user is connecting through a share).

Action Item: Talk with your IT professionals. Have them use the Microsoft Baseline Security Analyzer, a free download from Microsoft, or some other tool to show you how permissions are assigned. Two other useful tools are available at <u>www. sysinternals.com</u>. One is ShareEnum and the other is AccessEnum. If there are too many people with too much access, have the IT professional restrict access so each group of people can only see what they need to see.

CHAPTER 33

Licensing

Normally, software (and sometimes hardware and firmware) is licensed for use from the company that develops it. The companies that use the licensed products must ensure they are using them in a legal fashion. Development companies view any unauthorized use of their product as a crime, and they actively seek to verify compliance with their license agreements. Realize that your organization could be audited at any time for any reason, such as disgruntled employee "tattling" on you or just a random audit. You can find more information at www.bsa.org and by reviewing the licenses of your existing software and hardware.

A software audit can be a very traumatic experience unless your company has done adequate preparation in advance, in particular by gathering of all software certificates of authenticity as well as any other related documentation needed to prove that you have purchased all required licenses for every use of every product.

A common source of exposure to license violations is when employees bring software from home, including games and other software, and install it on company computers. If the software is installed on a company computer, you must have a license for the software on file.

Also as a side note, management needs to be informed that if they ever ask an IT professional to install an unlicensed program, even if only to "try it out for a few days," the manager needs to realize what a difficult position they are putting the IT professional in. If caught, that IT professional faces criminal charges as well as potentially losing his or her hard-earned technology certifications for life.

All machines should be scanned to determine if they have any unauthorized software installed on them, and if they do, the software should either be removed or a license obtained immediately. Consider using a tool such as www. systemhound.com to monitor your systems to be sure nothing is installed that isn't licensed.

Again, use Domain Policies to configure the network in such a way that end users are unable to install their own software on their workstations without the prior approval and/or assistance of the systems manager.

Action Item: Ensure that you have taken steps to be sure all required products are licensed and that the documentation is all in one place.

CHAPTER 34

Image Backup

Every company needs a strong backup strategy. I won't harp on this point for too long, because I know you are already aware of how crucial backups are. Plus, I learned my lesson a long time ago that harping does no good. So either you make good backups every day, take the media off site, and test the backups daily, or you don't. I strongly urge you to test the backups and carry the media off site daily.

With all that said, I do want to share with you something called "image backup." In my work with CEOs around the globe, I find that many executives are not aware of image backup, and many IT departments are not using it either.

As an executive, you lead a very busy life, and your technology needs to support the work you do. Anytime technology becomes an obstacle, people become frustrated. Most executives have at least one computer they rely upon on a daily basis. Hopefully they make daily backups of the machine. If they do, it is rarely an image backup. More likely, the executive doesn't backup at all, and if he or she does backup, it is some form of data file backup to capture their important work.

Let's face it. Computers crash. Here's what typically happens to executives who experience a crash and they have all their data backed up. They go to their IT department, give them their backup media and the computer, and say, "Fix this."

Since the executive isn't using image backup, the IT department has an enormous amount of work to perform:

- Wipe the computer's hard drive clean
- Reinstall Windows
- Reinstall the anti-virus
- Reinstall anti-spyware
- Reinstall the software firewall
- Now that the computer is protected, they can connect to the Internet
- Update Windows
- Update anti-virus
- Update anti-spyware
- Update the software firewall
- Restore the data from the backup media provided by the executive
- Reinstall Office
- Update Office
- Reinstall other programs the executive wants to use
- Update those extra programs
- Attempt to adjust the look and feel of the computer to be similar to what the executive prefers

- Test the system with the executive and correct the plethora of little issues that will of course show up

All this takes time and money. And it is all an unnecessary waste! If you only get fifty ideas from this book, please let this be one of those ideas.

You're actually much better off using something called image backup. With image backup, you not only backup your data, but you also backup every single thing in your computer. You backup Windows, the registry, all your programs, all the updates, all your data. All your personal settings...everything. And all this happens in one fell swoop. The backed up material is called an image, like a Polaroid camera.

I do an image backup every night—alternating between two different backup drives. That way, if my computer should ever crash, I can restore it very quickly, even if I lose one of the drives. Restoring from an image backup takes about twenty to forty minutes instead of forty to eighty hours.

Having an image backup is also useful when your company buys new computers. Chances are your IT professional already uses image backup in some capacity. For example, if you purchase six new computers, your IT team doesn't have to take the time to configure all six computers individually. In one sixth the time, they can configure just one computer, make an image backup, and use tools they know about to modify the image so it can be deployed on the other five computers. That way all six new computers are all the same.

So image backup is the way to go. If you're backing up any other way using file by file backup, switch to image backup. If you're not backing up at all, back up now.

I've had CEOs tell me that they use a laptop that their IT department keeps backed up for them. They say, "I don't need to back it up, because all my data is stored on the server." But if that laptop were to crash, it would still take way longer than that CEO wants to get the machine up and running again. That's why I encourage those IT professionals, "Please make an image of your CEO's drive. If it crashes, you can get the computer going again in twenty minutes."

Two good image backup solutions are Symantec Ghost from www.symantec.com or True Image from www.aconis.com. In you download either of these from the Internet, pay the small fee to have them ship you the CD. You definitely need the CD. When your computer crashes and you need to get it going again, you have to insert the product CD and boot the computer from that. With that said, make sure your computer actually will boot from the CD. Test it. Don't find out that it won't work the hard way.

You may choose to perform image backups of your servers too, using a tool such as Symantec LiveState Recovery, or www.UltraBac.com server image backup.

For backing up PDA and Smart Phone devices, consider an image backup tool such as Sprite Clone from www. spritesoftware.com. This tool can be used for backup as well as deployment to roll out exact images to many devices.

Action Item: At the very least, start using image backup on your own computer—the one that is the most important to your daily work. Purchase an external hard drive, throw away the backup software that is shipped with it, and purchase the latest release of Ghost. Have an IT professional set this up for you so your computer does automatic image backups daily. Test the backups. Do this today.

CHAPTER 35

Other Backup Options

For years, many organizations have opted to perform backups via a tape drive. Today, many companies are moving to hard drives and getting rid of their tapes. Why? Well, the tapes of today are very sophisticated and come with a computer chip on the tape cartridge. If that computer chip goes awry for whatever reason, the data on the tape is unusable. Unfortunately, Murphy's Law has set in a lot of times when people are backing up to tapes, and then when they try to restore, the tape won't work. But if you backup to a hard drive you don't have that problem.

Another advantage of doing backups to a hard drive is that if there's a hurricane, fire, or theft, and you have your tapes stored off site but you no longer have your tape drive, you can't access the data that's on the tapes until you get another tape drive. If your tape drive is an old model you have had for years, you may have a hard time quickly finding a tape drive that can read your tapes. When backing up to external hard drives, each drive is self contained. You can restore from the drive on any computer as long as you've installed your tape backup software and know the password to access the backup information.

So if being down for a week or two, or even a few days, would devastate your company, you need to reconsider your tape backup decision. If you still love tape backups and don't want to part with them, please purchase an extra tape drive unit and keep it somewhere off site. That way when you experience a disaster, you can at least have a tape drive handy to use to restore your data.

For many companies, a hard drive backup is the way to go. Realize that hard drive backups are faster too. With many of today's tape drive backups, the Tuesday backup has barely finished and it's time to start the Wednesday backup. Some companies in this situation of not having enough time to backup all the data during one night will revert to making full backups on weekends and then incremental or differential backups during the week. In the most simple terms, an incremental backup backs up the data that has changed since last backup, and a differential backup backs up the data changed since the most recent full backup. In the event of a restore of a large amount of data, using the incremental and differential backup methods can take significantly longer. Also, with more tape sets involved, there are more opportunities for Murphy's Law to destroy our ability to restore.

A strategy of making full backups every 24 hours is by far the preferred method of creating backups. Since a hard drive backup saves the data faster and restores it faster too, doing full backups is more feasible.

So if your IT professional comes to you and says, "We're getting rid of all our tapes and we're moving to hard drive backup," I want you to be able to say, "Yeah, I've heard of that before," instead of saying, "What?"

Other companies choose to backup their data to an outside source, such as to Iron Mountain at www.connected.com. The backup takes place over the Internet and the data is stored on the service provider's server.

Such an online backup service can backup whatever data you choose, including your Accounting software, corporate documents, paperless documents, etc. It's completely up to you what to backup.

One concern executives always bring up about using offline backup is, "Is our data secure?" Most of the companies offer you a method to encrypt your data so that only people you authorize can access it. Bring up the security question with your online backup provider. Also ask them how they will get you all of your data if you ever suffer a complete loss of data, as in a disaster. Often, performing a complete restore over an Internet connection would take too long and they will provide you with another alternative, such as sending DVDs using overnight shipping. If your provider is within driving distance, you can get your entire set of data even faster.

I've used an online backup system for years and am very happy with it. Remember that the online backup option is not an image backup. So I still backup my workstations every night with Symantec Ghost, and then I backup several times during the day to connected.com. In fact, after every two hours of work, I perform a backup unless I'm at 32,000 feet. That frequency of backup may seem excessive to some people, but I don't want to have to redo any work. I work hard enough and plenty of hours each week. I don't want my lack of backing up my data to add any hours to my workweek in the event of an unexpected loss of data.

Again, no matter what source you choose for your backup strategy, test it often. Too many companies have failed when they mistakenly thought they had a backup but didn't, and they suffered a catastrophic loss of data. I highly recommend you do formal testing and restores at least once a quarter.

The backup error log should be examined daily. Some IT professionals explain daily "failed backup" errors in their backup log with something like, "Oh, I know why that backup shows it has failed every day. It was caused by the ex-employee's old e-mail account that I haven't had time to delete yet." I express to them how important it is to delete the ex-employee's account, or exclude the folder, or do whatever needs to be done so that the backup log shows "successful" every day. This makes the daily examination of the backup error log much faster. You can glance to see the "successful" message in only seconds. Reviewing the logs takes much longer when the "backup failed" message appears, because then you have to spend time looking through the entire log to see if something unexpected is "failing."

If all that testing seems too complicated and you are very concerned to know if you even have the most basic of backups, try this experiment:

- Create and save a simple, non-important file on your network called something like "MyReallyImportantData.doc."
- Wait 24 hours and then delete the file
- Call IT and say, "Oh, my gosh. I've lost this file. Can you please get it back?" And then start the stopwatch to time how long it takes to get your file back.

This isn't the best or most scientific test in the world, but it will at least let you feel more confident that your organization is getting some kind of backup.

(Note that some IT professionals inform me that almost every day someone in their organization performs this test, "Uh, I've lost my file; can you get it back for me?" The hard part is that they often don't know the file's name or even where they saved it. This kind of detective work is often where IT professionals waste a lot of time!)

Action Item: Find out how frequently your organization performs backups, and how frequently your IT department tests the restore procedure. If your tape drive is too slow, consider moving to hard drive media. Also find out where the backup media is stored off site and make sure you feel comfortable with the security of the transport method and location.

CHAPTER 36

Disaster Recovery Plans

As we see in the news almost every day, all businesses need a Disaster Recovery Plan (DRP). Realize that a disaster can hit anyone at any time and can include such things as fire, theft, hurricane, long-term power outages, terrorist attacks, hacker attacks...the list is endless. Your plan needs to allow for the continuation of business in the event that one or more servers, and potentially even an entire site, becomes inoperative for any reason. The DRP includes provisions for rapid transfer to new servers and minimal (if any) downtime for users.

Whatever you do, please don't think that your business is immune from some sort of disaster. Every business is at risk. When I consult with companies, during the first visit my clients generally report something like: "We are going to start working on our DRP real soon." Thank goodness that at least some companies do have a DRP in place and test it regularly.

When it comes to disaster planning for your company's data, you have several options and levels of backup servers. As you move up the scale, you will invest more money in your DRP, and at the same time, you will experience less downtime in the event of a disaster. The key is to balance the cost of implementing the DRP with your needs. A simple way to determine a rough budget for your DRP is to calculate the money you will lose when your company is without a network and then multiply the costs times the percentage of likelihood of that disaster occurring. This gives you a rough budget for your DRP. To tune that amount, you can calculate different costs and likelihoods for being down an hour, a day, and a week. This gives you not only a more accurate amount, but also a better idea of how quickly the network needs to be up and running again.

With all this said, realize that you don't have to invest a lot into a DRP, but at the same time you need to invest enough to protect yourself appropriately.

At the bottom end of the DRP plans, at the very least, have a list of specifications for new servers that will be ordered in case you lose your existing servers. Make lists of the default builds of workstations in different areas and of your servers. Be sure to store these lists somewhere else in addition to on the network so that if the network is unavailable, you will still have access to the lists.

The next level up is to purchase cold standby servers. This is when you buy servers and have them off site. Then, if there is a disaster, you just move those servers on site, restore your backups, and then start going again. In some circumstances, the cold standby servers can be the "old servers" that were left over the last time you upgraded your servers. With this type of DRP, you can potentially be up and running again within the same day the disaster strikes. Your team will want to practice this restore process at least yearly.

If being down a day is unacceptable for you, then you will need a more advanced DRP. In that case, you have what's called collocation. That's when you have two sets of servers in more than one geographic location. Then, if any or all of your servers go down, the other servers just takes over. You may choose a relatively low-risk place for your second servers, such as the middle of Arizona. Other organizations that have offices in multiple locations just choose to use a secure room at a second office to house the standby servers.

The good news is that to save money, some solutions allow you to have a single "standby server" that can take on the load of more than one of your production servers in the event of a disaster. This way you save money, since you only need to buy one main server for your collocation site. The trade-off is that in the event of an emergency, your network will run much slower than normal. But at least you'll be running. The options are plentiful. For example, maybe your main office has eight servers, so you put four servers at your collocated site.

Blue Cross Blue Shield is one company that uses collocation. They actually have the collocation going with other call centers, and they practice the switch over once a week. When 9/11 occurred and one of the towers collapsed, one of the offices for Blue Cross Blue Shield was destroyed. Immediately, the collocation took place and that call center's calls were transferred to another location. When the new call center starting receiving the calls, they thought it was just the normal weekly test. Of course, they quickly learned the truth, but it just shows how smooth you want the server transfer to be in the event of a disaster.

With the collocation method, you would use a product such as DoubleTake as part of your plan. Then, as long as everything works right, there can potentially be no downtime at all. This investment in the DRP will be worthwhile if your business will experience large losses during a computer downtime.

Again, *you must test your disaster recovery plan regularly.* I was doing a security review recently and the CEO told me, "We have all this disaster recovery planning stuff in place, and we're paying a company to help us with it. But for us to test it, they want to charge us $10,000, so we've never tested it."

That's ridiculous! If you ever find yourself in a similar situation, tell the company that's "helping you" that you will move to another company to do the DRP for you if they're not going to let you test it at least once a year. Otherwise, you're not going to have faith that your plan will actually work should the need arise. Finally, realize that if your sole IT professional, or any member of your IT team, got seriously hurt and could not come to work for any length of time, that's a disaster too, and you need to have plan for such a scenario. Therefore, have great documentation of your system, including, but not limited to, the following:

- Network diagram
- Internet and WAN connectivity
- Administrative passwords
- List of vendors, consultants, and support with complete contact information

- Server and workstation configurations, including
  - IP Addresses
  - Information on remote offices and/or users
- Routine tasks such as resetting forgotten user passwords
- Backup / Restore procedures
- RAID array procedures

Without your IT professionals, your company would suffer a loss that could be just as great as what would occur in the event of a natural disaster that closed your company for several days. So have a plan for everything. While I hope you never need to enact your plan, I do want you to have one, just in case.

Action Item: If you have no firm DRP in place, then ensure that your organization actually sets a date within the next three months to implement a DRP. Use those three months to perform a downtime risk analysis, seek out options, and plan the DRP deployment. If you never set a date, then chances are you'll find yourself without a DRP for many more years to come, and that is a dangerous place to be.

CHAPTER 37

Physical Security

Your servers have to be kept under lock and key. If hackers were to ever get physical access to your servers, they can do an extraordinary amount of damage and often gain access to all your information. In some cases, the physical access need only be a few moments. So in regard to your building or office, you need to keep your company's servers and other IT equipment physically safe.

Be sure your servers, routers, and firewall are in an appropriate server room that is clean, cool, and closed. Consider installing an electronic lock of some kind that will allow you to track access to the server room.

It is also imperative to have adequate ventilation and air conditioning in the server room to keep the servers running at a cool temperature. Some IT professionals say they have to leave their server room's door open because it gets too hot in the room. Here's a simple solution for that: Purchase a portable air conditioning unit for your server room.

Workstation Security

Workstations, especially laptops, need to have full disk encryption in place. I know we talked about encryption earlier, but it's worth repeating here. As mentioned, encryption is when all the data on the hard drive is scrambled in such a way that it is useless to anyone except people who have the special "key" to unlock the data. That "key" may be something as simple as a fingerprint on the primary user's finger.

Earlier in the book I mentioned some inexcusable examples of organizations that lost laptops containing private information, and the information stored on those laptops was non-encrypted. Most new laptops come with a TPM, Trusted Platform Module, with a fingerprint reader and software that makes encryption a snap: easy to configure, free to obtain, and simple and fast for the end user to use.

Other tools that are wonderful for encryption include www.truecrypt.org and the BitLocker tool that is available in some versions of Microsoft Vista.

In addition to encrypting full drives, I also recommend that people encrypt important files, just in case someone ever sends an e-mail attachment containing the file to the wrong recipient by accident. Just keep in mind that many files can be decrypted using tools such as those found at www.lostpassword.com.

Also, before you discard any old computers or drives, erase them. Just because you think the computer or drive isn't worth fixing or upgrading doesn't mean a hacker can't fix it and see all your information. But if your full disk encryption is working properly, there will be no need to fully erase drives since nobody can access the information anyway.

Finally, consider installing LoJack on all your laptops. This way if your laptop is ever stolen, you can quickly get it back. LoJack is like the OnStar system for cars. If your laptop is stolen, you simply call LoJack and tell them. They can track where the laptop is using a GPS system and then the police can reclaim it for you. Other tools, such as www.cyberangel.com do something similar.

Action Item: Take an inventory of all portable computes and removable hard drives in your organization. Focus on making sure all of them are using full disk encryption, are protected by a recovery system such as LoJack for laptops, and have as little private data stored on them as possible.

CHAPTER 38

Wireless Security

Wireless networking technologies, such as WiFi, are a huge benefit for businesses as long as they're using their wireless correctly. Realize that providing free unencrypted wireless access at your place of business can be dangerous, even if that wireless network is on a separate network than your main network. For example, what if someone pulls into your parking lot after hours and performs illegal activities using your WiFi network? The police will come looking for you. As far as the police are concerned, the illegal activities happened over your network, so you are responsible. Some people say that they want to provide wireless for clients, customers, board members, and other visitors who come in. My answer is, "No." It's simply not worth the risk.

I recently did a security review at a car dealership that has WiFi for their customers. The premise is that if you're waiting there to get your car repaired, at least you can go online and get some work done or simply pass the time. One of the salespeople who works there is also a police officer at night. He told me a story of how he was walking through the service waiting room one day. He saw an older man sitting there working on a computer. The man was there for a very long time. He got suspicious, so he asked the service manager when the man's car would be ready. As it turns out, they weren't even servicing his car. This man was on the Internet engaging in some illegal activities. He was using the car dealership's WiFi, because he thought he'd have less risk of getting caught using someone else's network, and he didn't want his online activity to get traced back to his house. Of course, he didn't figure that an off-duty police officer would be working at the dealership.

As a side note, that man who was using the dealership's WiFi is in prison right now.

If you do want to provide access to visitors, then require each of them to have individual usernames and passwords to access your system. Set their accounts to expire after a certain amount of time. If you feel that is too much trouble, then at the very least get yourself a hot tub timer. Have an electrician install it and have the guest wireless access point hooked to it. Now when you start your meeting, or when you have a client on site who wants to use your connection, you crank the timer to 30 or 60 minutes. That access point is available that long, and then it shuts off automatically. If you need more time, go over and give it another crank, just like you would with a hot tub. But do not leave that access point open day and night for anyone to log on and cause problems.

Using WiFi for employees to have access to your network is another matter entirely. And this can be just as dangerous if it isn't protected. But since we are talking about employee computers here, your IT professionals will be able to take the necessary steps on the client computers to make sure they are much more secure.

If you currently have a wireless network just for your employees, make sure your IT professionals have done what is necessary to increase the security. Some of this is technical, but your IT people will know what it means:

- Update the firmware in the WAP to the most recent version.

- For encryption, instead of using the outdated WEP, be sure to use WPA or WPA2 immediately. Be sure to use a long pass-phrase. Also, know that Cisco LEAP authentication can be hacked by a tool called ASLEAP due to a weakness in Microsoft's MS-CHAPv2 standard used by LEAP. Authentication that is more secure includes WPA, WPA2, EAP-FAST, and PEAP.

- Using a VPN for your wireless devices is even better for encryption. Ask your vendor to disable Aggressive Mode IKE since there are tools that can break the IKE pre-shared keys used by IKE/IPsec.

- Consider disabling the SSID broadcast to reduce exposure of the wireless network to casual observers. Disabling the SSID broadcast doesn't help security much for a determined hacker.

- Consider implementing MAC filtering to restrict WiFi access to only the computers you approve to allow to connect. WPA encryption is much more effective than using MAC filtering.

- Periodic password changes with both a minimum and maximum password age.

- Consider disabling DHCP on the wireless segment to make it more difficult for users to connect, although again, WPA or WPA2 is more effective than this strategy.

- Unless there is a really great reason to enable it, be sure to leave remote administration disabled. If you need outside consultants to be able to configure the WAP remotely, they could use a VPN or some other method to control the access point.

Finally, perform regular scans to be sure there are no unauthorized, and therefore insecure, wireless access points on the network.

Wireless networking can save a lot of money if it means less copper needs to be pulled through walls in a building. In some cases, some companies opt to avoid wireless, but if you choose to use it, now you know steps to help keep it more secure.

Action Item: Download the free tool Net Stumbler from www.stumbler.net to see if there are wireless networks available at your office. Visit with your IT professionals about the security of the networks.

CHAPTER 39

Endpoint Security

Endpoint security is another of my favorite things. Many companies today have remote users who access the network. Telecommuting is a great thing and I encourage all companies to consider offering it. Just remember that if those computers your employees have at home or on the road are infected, they're going to infect the network.

Realize that those home computers fall under the umbrella of your internal IT department, which can create a lot of work, because you either have to outsource to A&B Computer downtown on the corner to go to all of your employees' houses and make sure their computers are safe on a regular basis, or you have to get your IT professionals to remotely log in and make sure they're safe. Another option is to use endpoint security.

Endpoint security is a combination of the firewall components and a special software program that gets installed on each of the remote computers that will connect to the main office.

Here's how it works: Every time a remote user connects to your firewall, your firewall stops them and makes sure their computer is okay. If their computer is not okay, they're not allowed in. On top of that, endpoint security will go to work and make their computer okay, with no human intervention. That means your IT department doesn't have to do anything. They don't even have to know what's going on. The user hooks up, finds out their computer isn't safe, the firewall doesn't let them in, the program automatically makes their computer safe, and then they're allowed in.

Think about all the money you can save with this one technology. Now you can see why I get excited about endpoint security.

Action Item: If you have employees who remotely access the network, make sure you have some sort of endpoint security in place. Talk with your IT Professional about it today.

CHAPTER 40

Commit to IT Accountability

Congratulations for making it through to this point in the book. I know that the material is somewhat technical, but now you are better prepared to provide oversight to your IT team.

Realize, though, that in order to make anything discussed in this book work, you need to commit to IT accountability. Without your commitment to this, it won't happen.

Unfortunately, many executives cite lack of knowledge as to why they don't have any IT accountability in place. They don't find IT exciting, so they wait until IT has a fire to put out before they deal with it. Others claim that they feel intimidated by IT. They say, "IT treats me like a moron." But that's no longer an excuse for you.

Additionally, some companies simply tolerate such things as insecure passwords, users installing any software they want, and letting star performers slide in terms of security issues. They also fail to provide IT security awareness training to their employees. But having a culture of "we trust everyone" or "we are a family business and don't want to be big brother watching our employees" ultimately will come back to bite a company.

So how do you truly empower yourself in terms of IT? Simple. You get an IT audit. Think about it, companies regularly get accounting audits. Why not IT audits?

Even better, have an IT vital systems review that takes the audit to the next level. Find out what your organization needs, and let an experienced person lead your IT team towards being in compliance with IT best practices.

Ask yourself how much it would cost if your network goes down today and one of your top three customers leaves you because you couldn't serve them. That is a real problem. What if you have a loss of secure information from your server? What if you have to provide credit protection services? What if your company's secrets get stolen? What if your company image is damaged because something disgusting is found on your servers and it gets out? How expensive would that be to you?

Please take charge of IT security at your organization. Designate a person in your organization to be responsible for IT security and get an audit. I see a lot companies make the mistake of trying to fix their IT security issues themselves and then have a vital systems security review. That's the backwards way of doing it. Have someone come in, review your systems, mentor your IT professionals, and show you the best practices. You'll actually save money doing it this way than if you waste a lot of time and money trying to figure out what's wrong on your own.

If you have an IT department and they feel offended that you want to have an IT audit, explain to them that you don't expect them to be an expert in everything, just as you wouldn't expect your general practitioner to perform heart surgery. It's okay to get other people involved. Basically you're trying to help them by having someone else come in who your IT professionals can communicate with, and just be an extra set of eyes. Be sure to tell them that they're not under any judgment. Your IT people may be the "best of the best." That isn't the issue. You just want to help them grow even better. The goal is simply to take the company's IT utilization to the next level.

Think of it like Cliff Notes for your IT professional. Now they don't have to go out to IT security training, unless they want to. Instead, they can have someone else come in and look at the situation and point out alternatives.

A typical security audit involves weeks or months, and it's very expensive. For most small and medium sized business, it's overkill. The much better solution is the IT vital systems security review.

In addition to examining the current situation, the IT vital systems security review is a mentoring process, so that your IT professionals learn to fish, so to speak. Even if your IT professionals are outsourced, they learn to fish and they learn how to take better care of you, and that's a very powerful thing. That's also a much higher return on your investment.

When it comes to finding the right reviewer for you, you need to ask a few questions.

1. Is the person independent? If this person sells Cisco routers, then he's probably going to tell you that you need a Cisco router to be more secure. Even if he is telling the truth, you're going to have some doubt. So make sure there's no doubt.

2. Is it more than just a penetration test? Are they just going to try to break in? Anybody can break into anything, given enough time and energy. You're better off having someone come and help you protect your system from that happening.

3. Are they going to give you a road map detailing how to take your company to the next level? You don't want to have to monitor these people, because that's not what you do. You do executive stuff. So you'd want to be able to hand this off to someone else.

As a side benefit to the audit or review, other IT mysteries you've been having will get solved. It's hard for me to think of a security review where we didn't find out other challenges people were having with their technology that weren't security related. We can then give the best practices to get around those problems.

If you outsource your IT, then you would outsource your security review to another firm that's totally separate from your existing IT outsource provider. Your IT company should be very open to that. If they're terrified about it, then that should be a clue to you about your choice in IT provider.

Overall, I find that almost everybody, including the IT professionals, is open to the review. It's very rare that people say, "No, no, I don't want this." Some IT professionals are nervous at first, but once they understand that we're on the same team and that an audit is about fixing things and helping them, then they open up and are very appreciative. Many are even eager, especially since they know they will be the "heroes" once everything is implemented.

Since this is about "going for the long-haul," incorporate IT metrics into your meetings too. Invite IT staff to your meetings. Make sure they're keeping you updated. Talk about the IT issues with them. Get that open communication going.

Finally, automate, centralize, and watch. You want your IT security to be taken care of automatically, because the more trouble it is to take care of your system, the more likely your system won't be taken care of.

Back in the Introduction of this book, we discussed briefly the concept of ensuring that IT professionals aren't being interrupted by emergencies all day long. One of the biggest keys to getting closer to such an environment is through the use of central management and daily checklists.

Here's a simple daily checklist your IT professional or designed person can do each morning. Just like pilots perform a pre-flight check before every flight, every morning someone needs to spend 10 minutes verifying items such as:

- Backup report(s) – check for any errors
- WSUS – see list of machines needing updates

- Anti-Virus
  - Scanned all files within 24 hours
  - Updated signature file
  - Anti-Virus program version
- Anti-Spyware
  - Scanned all files within 24 hours
  - Updated signature file
  - Anti-Spyware program version
- Personal Firewall
  - Software firewall program version
  - Any errors on any machines
- RAID array utilities – verify integrity of RAID arrays
- Main Firewall error log
- Event viewers on servers
- Any other appropriate checks

If any problems are discovered, you can correct them before they escalate in severity or lead to more problems.

The point of all this is to help you protect your assets. I've seen the bad things that can happen. Please protect yourselves and protect to your organization by committing to everything you learned in this book.

I hope you now feel better informed about your IT security issues and have useful tools and actionable items that you can put to work immediately.

Here are two questions I'd like you to answer now:

1. What will you do to put all your action steps into action?
2. Knowing what you know, on a scale of one to ten, with ten being the most secure, how secure do you think your company is right now? Whatever number you're thinking, I challenge you to get to an eleven.

As you likely already know, handoff is not enough. If you just hand this book to your IT professionals and tell them "Do this," that's not enough. They are so busy already that these issues will always be put off until tomorrow. That's why you have to stay on top of them and offer to help often. Hold them accountable and provide appropriate training. Schedule an IT vital systems security review so the reviewer to mentor them.

The good new is, with the help of a qualified IT professional, you *can* do everything outlined in this book. Others before you have done it, and you're just as capable. So go out there and get started on your action items. You'll be glad you did.

About the Author

Mike Foster is the founder and CEO of the Foster Institute. Mike started programming computers during the 1970s.

For twelve years, Mike was the CEO of his own very successful company and supported insurance companies, banks, law offices, investment and trading companies, accounting offices, medical facilities, agricultural companies, car dealerships, rental companies, city/county/state government agencies and offices, and organizations of almost every type.

In 1997 Mike allowed the company to operate without his physical presence, as he began a professional speaking and consulting career that has taken him traveling to deliver more than 1,000 presentations and serve clients in the USA, Canada, South Africa, England, Scotland, Ireland, Australia, and New Zealand.

Over the years, Mike has encountered dozens of breaches of company network security. He came to the aid of an East Coast company whose corporate firewall had been disconnected because the IT department "couldn't figure it out." And he helped the CEO whose computer was taken over by hackers in the hour that his teenage son was "helping out Dad" with the computer. Another company thought they were making back-ups, but thanks to Mike, realized that they hadn't in years.

Mike Foster is accustomed to skillfully providing CEOs with solutions to their high-tech issues. He has been well received in the U.S. and many other countries. *USA Today*, *Forbes Magazine*, *Kiplinger Letter*, *Entrepreneur Magazine*, *Insight Magazine* and *Atlanta Business Monthly* have featured Mike's work. Mike often works as an "interpreter" between IT departments and management, providing important and insightful results for both groups. Organizations that have benefited from Mike's talents include:

- Amazon.com
- American Express
- Blue Cross/Blue Shield
- The CEO Institute
- Chase Manhattan Bank
- City of Houston 911
- Dallas Area Rapid Transit
- Dell
- Eli Lilly
- Honeywell
- Marriott International
- Microsoft
- Perot Systems
- U.S. Marines
- U.S. Postal Service

Mike's speaking covers a range of topics. To highly technical audiences, Mike presents workshops on installing, troubleshooting, and supporting operating systems such as Microsoft Windows Server 2003, application software such as Microsoft SQL Server 2000, and infrastructures including TCP/IP routing. At the other end of the spectrum, Mike uses his uncanny ability to explain complex topics in easy-to-understand ways in order to help non-technical audiences better utilize technology for productivity and profit, and make networks more secure. In addition to technology topics, Mike also enjoys presenting inspirational messages during keynote speeches.

In addition to his extensive experience and education in computer technology, Mike has earned several certifications during his career including:

- A+ Certified Computer Technician
- i-Net+ CompTIA Internet Professional
- ᵃ Network+ CompTIA Network Technician
- CCNA: Cisco Certified Network Associate
- MCSE: Microsoft Certified Systems Engineer
- MCP+I: Microsoft Certified Professional + Internet

Mike is independent and provides objective recommendations based upon industry standard best practices, his own extensive training, discoveries, and observations made while consulting with other firms, and his own years of experience.

For more information about how Mike can help your company, contact him via email at mike@fosterinstitute.com and visit his web site www.FosterInstitute.com. For more information about IT Vital Systems Reviews see www.KeepMyNetorkSafe.com

Mike Foster provides practical insights and relevant Network Security solutions and IT Best Practices that you can use to help protect your business!

Imagine how much money, time and credibility your organization would lose *per hour* if your network was compromised. . .

Plus add-in the *intangibles* that will be lost when you have to notify your clients or employees that you've had a security breach and that their private data has been released to identity thieves.

Have you ever considered . . .

- *how your customers would react if you could not serve them for a few days because your network was hacked and stopped working?*
- *how much revenue you'd lose if one of your top customers decided to go with another IT supplier?*
- *what the consequences would be if you suffered a security breach and released confidential information to competitors, identity thieves, etc.?*

You and your IT staff may *think* your network is secure... but what would it be worth to you to know for sure?

Businesses today face ever-expanding corporate networks, growth in the use of mobile devises, and real risks pertaining to security and protection inefficiencies. This leads to an urgent need to proactively plan and protect corporate interests—IT is of crucial and strategic importance. Mike Foster, President of Foster Institute, provides practical insights and relevant IT Network Security solutions and IT Best Practices that you can use to protect your business.

In 90% of companies Mike has reviewed they all had at least one major "security bleeding artery" that they weren't aware of before Mike's review. Often these were companies where the IT people insisted *no* security vulnerabilities would be found.

Mike offers customized security review options to fit your company's needs.

Find out how you can help you protect your business, find potential security problems and get real solutions with a Network Security and IT Best Practices Review!

Contact Mike Foster today!
1-800-657-7107 or (214) 269-1204
www.KeepMyNetworkSafe.com
mike@KeepMyNetworkSafe.com

ATTN CEOS, EXECUTIVES & IT LEADERS! Imagine your IT department running like a well-oiled machine, with your network secure, IT best practices implemented, lines of communication wide open, and misunderstandings a thing of the past . . . .

Mike Foster's
Super-Tech IT Best Practices Workshop
A 2-Day Workshop for IT Professionals

The Super-Tech "Best Practices" Workshop isn't some rah-rah motivational speech filled with theory and conjuncture. Instead, this workshop offers IT "super-techs" and their managers real "best practices" that will enhance and update their knowledge of current IT security threats, and improve their communication and teach them how to get more done in less time!

This workshop is the fast track for IT professionals to end the nightmare of putting out fires all the time and be caught up on all of the IT projects.

Your IT professional will leave with the tools and education they need to succeed in their job, keep the company network safe from security breeches, learn timely and up-to-date IT best practices, maximize their productivity, and increase your company's bottom-line results!

Get all the Details and Register today!
1-800-657-7101 or 214-269-1204
www.SuperTechEvent.com
Email: Mike@KeepMyNetworkSafe.com